Allan Sweeney was initially sentenced to life in prison in 1975 at the age of nineteen, after he mutilated and stabbed to death a female neighbour while her two children slept. The sexual motive of the attack was clearly established at his trial, and a psychiatrist testified that "given similar circumstances, if such were possible, the same thing could happen again."

The information was not conveyed to penitentiary officials—Sweeney was recommended for day parole after nine and a half years because he was a "model prisoner."

Then, in 1985, Sweeney was granted full parole at a halfway house. After numerous reports that he had been drinking and taking drugs, his parole was suspended for one month. Fifteen days after his release, at one o'clock in the morning, the lone female staffer at the halfway house telephoned her supervisor to report that Sweeney had returned late and was acting strange.

It is believed to be the last phone call she made before she was raped, mutilated, and stabbed to death.

CRIMINAL NEGLECT

Why Sex Offenders Go Free

Dr. W. L. Marshall
&
Sylvia Barrett

SEAL BOOKS
McClelland-Bantam, Inc.
Toronto

CRIMINAL NEGLECT

A Seal Book / published by arrangement with
Doubleday Canada Limited

PRINTING HISTORY
Doubleday Canada edition published 1990
Seal edition / March 1992

ISBN 0-770-42487-2

Seal Books are published by McClelland-Bantam, Inc. Its trademark, consisting of the words "Seal Books" and the portrayal of a
seal, is the property of McClelland-Bantam, Inc., 105 Bond Street,
Toronto, Ontario M5B 1Y3, Canada. This trademark has been duly
registered in the Trademark Office of Cananda. The trademark
consisting of the words "Bantam Books" and the portrayal of a
rooster is the property of and is used with the consent of Bantam
Books, 666 Fifth Avenue, New York, New York 10103. This trademark has been duly registered in the Trademark Office of Canada
and elsewhere.

PRINTED IN CANADA
COVER PRINTED IN U.S.A.

UNI   0 9 8 7 6 5 4 3 2 1

Contents

Acknowledgements   vii

Introduction   ix

1   Tragic Failures: Duane Taylor and Melvin Stanton   1

2   Bureaucratic Bungling and Indifference   22

3   Behind the Walls   44

4   Profile of a Sex Offender   68

5   The Motives of Sex Offenders   85

6   Shattering the Myths   107

7   Turning a Blind Eye   118

8   The Victims   139

9   The Link to Pornography   154

10   The Case for Treatment   179

11   Beyond the Short-term Answers   198

Notes   211

Index   213

Acknowledgements

I WOULD LIKE to thank my family, Nina and Liam Marshall, who gave me the help and support that allowed me to get started in this strange career of treating sex offenders. Their indulgence and constant belief in me permitted my limited wits their fullest expression. Their love and compassion have helped me over the years from burning out in this taxing business. I owe them a debt I will never be able to repay. More recently, Allana and Jean have offered similar support, for which I am grateful.

My students over the years have always been inspiring, most particularly Zindel Segal, Chris Earls, Janel Gauthier, Bonnie Hays, Marilyn Christie, and Juliet Darke. Without my dear friends and colleagues at the clinic, Howard Barbaree, Wayne Westfall, Jill Milligan, Tony Eccles, Sharon Hodkinson, and Krista Payne, I would not have survived these many years.

Finally, I wish to thank my many patients who have helped me learn whatever it is I know.

W.L.M.

TO MY DAUGHTER Stephanie, who stoically accepted second place to this book over the past year and made many related sacrifices, I owe my greatest debt.

I am indebted as well to my mother, Betty, and to the rest of my family for their constant encouragement, and for never once suggesting that I get a "real job."

To the many friends who have provided unending moral support and practical assistance over the year—particularly Anne Kershaw, Jane Derby, Sharron Kusiar, Valerie Voight, David Lees, and Phil Hess—I am also deeply grateful.

Lastly, I would like to thank our editor, Shelley Tanaka, for her discerning questions, her equanimity and her friendship.

S.B.

Introduction

SEXUAL ASSAULT IS a subject that makes everyone feel uncomfortable. For some it evokes painful memories. For others, fear or anger or guilt. Its vile nature makes it one of the most loathed crimes, but it is rarely a topic of everyday conversation. Many people would rather not have to deal with the issue. When we seek refuge from our discomfort in denial, however, when we disavow the victims and the offenders, we perpetuate the problem. And it is widespread.

One in four females and one in eight males in Canada are sexually assaulted—eighty percent of them before they reach the age of twenty-one. Indeed, the frequency of sexual crimes against women and children makes them banal: With few exceptions, they are accorded a mere inch or two of space in newspaper accounts and ignored by other news media.

Recently, however, sexual assault victims have begun to break the silence that surrounds this most under-reported of crimes. In unprecedented numbers, they are now lodging complaints about recent assaults and about offences that occurred years ago. And governments are listening. The public revelations of one victim launched an enquiry in Newfoundland in 1989 into the sexual abuse fifteen years earlier of boys at Mount Cashel orphanage in St. John's— an investigation that sent shock waves across the country. But merely recognizing the problem of sexual assault is not enough. We have written this book because we believe that if we are even to begin to reduce the incidence of rape and child molestation, we must talk openly and frankly about all of these crimes, not just the most sensational of them. And if we are to have any hope of eradicating them, we must understand not only their facade but their origins.

Sexual assault is a complex issue that lends itself to being scrutinized from a single point of view. But dissecting the subject does not promote an understanding of it. This book looks at who is victimized and what they suffer. It considers the entire range of offenders— from sexual killers to teachers who molest their students to men who rape their own daughters— and what motivates them to commit their crimes. It explores how the criminal justice system and society in general deal with the victims and offenders. It examines treatment programs for sex offenders and measures their benefits to society. Finally, it suggests that the very root of this relentless epidemic lies in our attitudes.

Bill Marshall is a psychologist who has been treating and assessing sex offenders for twenty years. He was co-director of the treatment program for sex offenders at Kingston Penitentiary at its inception in 1973; eleven years later, he set up a second program at the prison for offenders with subnormal intelligence.

For seventeen years, Marshall has been co-director of the Kingston Sexual Behaviour Clinic, an out-patient facility for sex offenders, primarily child molesters, from southeastern Ontario. The clinic, which is currently supported by a grant from the Ontario Ministry of Correctional Services, assesses approximately two hundred offenders a year and treats fifty to sixty.

In 1989, Marshall and Howard Barbaree, the clinic's other director, were awarded a grant from the Correctional Service of Canada to begin treating sex offenders at Warkworth Institution, a penitentiary in eastern Ontario, making it only the fourth federal prison to establish a treatment program for incarcerated rapists and pedophiles.

Collectively, Marshall's experiences have afforded him a rare understanding of why the present systems and institutions dealing with sex offenders fail. As a woman and a mother, journalist Sylvia Barrett shares his concern about the very real threat posed to all women and children by offenders who either escape detection and/or conviction or are incarcerated but receive little or not treatment before they are released back into society.

The authors began work on the book shortly after an inquest began into the death of Tema Conter, a Toronto fashion buyer. The twenty-five-year-old woman was accosted at the door of her uptown apartment as she was leaving for work at 8:00 A.M. on a Wednesday. Her assailant was a sex offender on a temporary absence pass from a federal penitentiary, who had escaped from a halfway house nearby.

The events that led to the brutal rape and murder of this young woman by Melvin Stanton, a man who had previously raped three women and beaten to death his teenage girlfriend, painfully illustrate the flaws that currently exist in our penal-parole system, from the bureaucratic bungling and indifference that has contributed to many sexually motivated murders and rapes by released offenders to the lack of adequate treatment provided for these men either inside or outside the prison walls.

The book describes how the penal-parole system works—how the parole board determines which offenders it will release and how they will be supervised in the community— while providing a glimpse into what goes on behind the walls of Kingston Penitentiary, Canada's oldest and most notorious prison. Here, Clifford Olson and thirty-three other men spend twenty-three hours a day locked inside cramped cells in a range known as "protective custody within protective custody," as staff at the regional treatment centre decide which sex offenders imprisoned in Ontario and the Atlantic provinces will receive therapy.

The ineffectual system governing the treatment and release of incarcerated rapists and pedophiles is only part of the reason that sexual crimes continue unabated. Society's attitudes play the greatest role. These are reflected in myriad cases involving the coverup of crimes by professionals such as Robert Noyes, a British Columbia teacher, who molested children at five schools over a fifteen-year period; in the number of sexual assault allegations that are deemed unfounded by the police; and in the blatant bias against sexual assault victims evident in countless judicial rulings.

The conspiracy of denial goes beyond those directly involved with sexual crimes, however. Society in general aids and abets sex offenders through its laissez-faire attitudes towards violence in the media, sex in advertising and, especially pornography. It also places women and children at greater risk of being victimized and allows offenders to go free by clinging to myths of the stereotypical offender and the blame worthy victim. The fact is that sex offenders are not fundamentally different from the rest of us; nor are the victims an isolated group.

The pervasiveness of sexual assault makes it everyone's problem. While that is a cause for concern, it is also a cause for hope because, although there are no easy answers, the power to greatly reduce sexual crimes lies in the hands of average Canadians. We need only to accept the responsibility to do so, and look beyond the short-term solutions to the significant changes that must be undertaken if society is to empower, and thereby protect, women and children. The time is now.

CRIMINAL NEGLECT

1

Tragic Failures:
Duane Taylor and
Melvin Stanton

WHEN DUANE TAYLOR arrived at Kingston Penitentiary at the age of seventeen, he was no stranger to institutional living. Like many of the young men entering the limestone fortress that holds some of Canada's most notorious criminals, Taylor was a graduate of a long string of reform schools and group homes.

Shortly after his eighth birthday, he and an older brother were banished from their southern Ontario home to a reform school a two-hour drive away. They had been playing hookey. For all but a few months thereafter, Taylor remained in some form of custody. Either years later, in 1977, while he was a resident at a group home near Peterborough, Ontario, he was caught trying to rape a four-year-old girl he had led into the bushes at a baseball game. It wasn't his first attack on

1

children. But this time, Taylor was tried in adult court and sentenced to four years in a federal penitentiary.

Interviewed behind bars by a National Film Board crew a couple of days after his arrival at Kingston Penitentiary (KP), the babyfaced teenager looked decidedly out of place. "Why are you in here?" a reporter asked him, referring to the cramped protective custody cell that would be his home for the next couple of years.

"Just for my protection," the youth mumbled.

"What do you mean, your protection?"

"Well, my age, like that."

"Do you feel that being in here is going to help you with your problems?" the interviewer continued.

"Yeah. I think they will," the inmate replied.

"How about before, when you were in other places, did those places help you with your problems?"

"No. Not much."

The help Taylor needed would not be found in prison either.

The illiterate and borderline retarded pedophile was twenty-one years old the first time he was let out of prison. He will be at least forty-six years old the next time.

Eleven days after his release in 1981, Taylor took a neighbour's two year old daughter into his rooming house in downtown Kingston, viciously raped and sodomized her, and then smothered her to death. He is now serving a life sentence with no chance of parole for twenty-five years. His story is a classic example of how the criminal justice system, and society generally, has failed to protect women and children from sex offenders— and offenders from themselves.

At his first trial, both a psychiatrist and the sentencing judge predicted that Taylor would repeat his crime; the judge recommended that the youth receive treatment to correct his deviant behaviour after he served his sentence.

The opportunity for help would actually present itself much sooner. Kingston Penitentiary was the first of four federal prisons across Canada to establish special treatment programs for sex offenders. And psychologists at the institution had been conducting individual and group therapy sessions for rapists and pedophiles for several years by the time Taylor arrived. After assessing the inmate for two months, the staff determined that he had strong sexual preferences for children over adults and for male children over female children; he displayed an equal preference for consenting and forced sex. Ultimately, however, they decided Taylor "did not possess the intellectual capacity" to benefit from their program. No other treatment arrangements were made.

For the next two and a half years, Taylor spent most of his time alone in a box-like cell outfitted with a metal bed and desk, a sink and an open toilet, protected from other inmates who would have abused him both because of his young age and because he was a sex offender. Like the majority of inmates confined to their cells most of the time, Taylor created no problems in prison. On September 2, 1980, after he had served two-thirds of his sentence, he was released on mandatory supervision.

Sex offenders with fixed sentences, like all federal penitentiary inmates, are eligible for day parole after they have served one-sixth of their prison term and for full parole after they have completed one-third. Whether they are granted either day or full parole, and the conditions of that parole, is determined by the parole board, whose members are political appointees. The decision is made at a hearing attended by at least two board members, who interview the inmate and consider his criminal and institutional records, any psychological reports, and the recommendations of his case management team, which comprises a parole officer and a penitentiary classification officer.

Offenders denied parole, but whose behaviour behind bars has been good, are automatically released from prison under mandatory supervision after they have served two-thirds of their sentences. Prior to 1970, they were discharged at that point with no supervision at all. Now inmates let out on mandatory supervision meet with a parole officer on the same basis as those granted parole—a preset schedule which gradually eases from a minimum of once every two weeks to once a month or, in the case of offenders serving life sentences, to once a year. Inmates who breach the terms of their mandatory supervision can be returned to prison but, in most cases, they can again earn one-third off their remaining sentences.

Since 1986, the parole board has had the power to detain, through a process called gating, any inmate it considers to be particularly dangerous. His release is delayed until his entire sentence has been served; then, however, the board cannot order the offender to be supervised in any manner when he finally is discharged. The gating legislation was not in effect when Taylor was eligible for mandatory supervision. He left that day for Toronto, where he was to live in a halfway house and look for a job.

A month earlier, a report by a penitentiary classification officer had warned: "Prognosis poor. To date inmate Taylor appears to the writer as not yet developing insight into his abnormal behaviour. His release plan lacks depth and subject will require close supervision and extensive assistance if he is to succeed."

Taylor didn't succeed. His first brush with freedom lasted only two weeks. He was forced to leave St. Leonard's halfway house after one night when the other residents discovered he was a sex offender. His parole officer found him a room at the YMCA, but he disappeared the next day. The following day, he was located in his hometown east of Toronto and was admitted to D'Arcy Developmental Centre in Cobourg, Ontario, an institution for retarded adults. Again, he ran away. He was found and returned to the centre. However, his tenure there ended abruptly when he was seen choking another resident and threatening him with his fists. There were also reports that he had made sexual advances to a female resident.

His mandatory supervision was revoked and Taylor was sent back to Kingston Penitentiary. For the next eleven months, his Kingston parole officer worked diligently to find him suitable accommodation and treatment. It was a difficult task. D'Arcy wouldn't take him back. Similar institutions in Edgar, Ontario, and in Kingston didn't want him. Halfway houses across Ontario turned him down. Even the Salvation Army, citing danger to both the public and the inmate, would offer only temporary refuge in its Kingston hostel.

In July 1981, one month before Taylor was due for release again, his parole officer approached Bill Marshall about the possibility of developing an individual treatment program for the inmate. Marshall was one of three professionals who had set up the sex offender program at Kingston Penitentiary in the mid-1970s, and he had been treating sex offenders outside prisons for twelve years. He assessed Taylor, concluded he was treatable, and agreed to treat him. However, both the federal correctional service and the provincial medicare program refused to pay for the therapy, each claiming it was the other's responsibility.

As a result of his assessment, which included measuring Taylor's penile erections in response to various visual stimuli, Marshall wrote the parole officer: "The chances of him offending against children are at the moment quite high, and I would not recommend release under anything but the most rigorously enforced supervision. . . . He needs considerable training in various areas as well as a treatment program aimed at reducing his aberrant sexual interests. Although he appears to be of low intelligence, this is not a serious obstacle to treatment of this kind."

Marshall ended his letter: "It is a disgrace that such an individual, who is a prime candidate for behavioural change, was left untreated during his stay in the penitentiaries to be now released to offend again against some innocent child."

August 10, the date for Taylor's inevitable return to the community, grew alarmingly closer. With the possibility for an individualized treatment program ruled out, Taylor's parole officer stepped up her search for help. Finally, three opportunities arose. Horizon House, an Ottawa halfway house, reluctantly agreed to accept Taylor for five days so he could be assessed at Royal Ottawa Hospital for possible entry into a treatment program there. Whitby Psychiatric Hospital, in southern Ontario, consented to take him for a conditional three-month assessment period in the fall. And Kingston Psychiatric Hospital offered to place him in a work-training program later that year.

On July 31, 1981, the three options were telexed to the National Parole Board. All were approved. On August 10, Taylor was given a second chance at freedom.

The Ottawa plan quickly fell through when Taylor failed to cooperate in his initial interview at Royal Ottawa Hospital. On August 13, he was back in Kingston. The Whitby Psychiatric Hospital couldn't take him until September 2. The Salvation Army agreed to feed him twice a day, but officials there said he could only stay at their downtown hostel until other accommodation could be found—a maximum of five days.

On August 18, Taylor moved into a Kingston rooming house. He had only two weeks to wait until he could be admitted to the Whitby hospital. He didn't make it.

His regular parole officer teamed up with a second officer to provide intense supervision. In the eight days that Taylor was on the streets of Kingston, they met with him and talked to him by telephone a total of twenty-one times. They took him to the city police department to be photographed and viewed by available members of the force. They even insisted that Taylor sign an undertaking to stay away from children, although a handwritten entry on the officers' activity sheet dated August 14 acknowledged the futility of the gesture. It reads: "'Not To Have Contact With Children' seems to be useless as Taylor doesn't seem to comprehend seriousness of situation." A similar notation on August 17 says: "Remind Taylor again re: children. Although he says he will not approach children, it is doubtful he will avoid kids."

On Friday, August 21, at 6:30 P.M., the parole supervisors had their last contact with Taylor. As requested, he called one of them at home to make plans to meet on Saturday. He had spent the day, as arranged, moving furniture for a man he had met in the park and said he was happy to have earned some money. There was no indication of what was to follow.

Just over an hour later, Taylor picked up April Morrison, a quiet, happy-go-lucky two-year-old girl, who was trailing her older brothers from a nearby park to her modest clapboard home, two doors down from Taylor's rooming house. Before dozens of children with flashlights and bicycles joined adults on foot and in cars to begin searching the working-class neighbourhood, Taylor had what he later described as "fun" with the little girl. When she started crying and bleeding, he panicked, and silenced her by sitting on her face until she suffocated.

In a Newmarket, Ontario, courtroom a year later, Taylor pleaded guilty to a charge of first-degree murder. In sentencing him to life imprisonment with no possibility of parole for twenty-five years, Mr. Justice John O'Driscoll of the Ontario Supreme Court described the pedophile as "literally a time bomb waiting to explode" and recommended that he receive psychiatric treatment, psychological treatment, and any other kind of treatment that would help him while he was in prison.

"To leave him the way he is for twenty-five years and then turn him loose is not very sensible," the judge remarked.

Within three days of April Morrison's murder, officials at the Correctional Service of Canada (CSC) launched an internal inquiry to determine what had happened, a standard practice following any sensational incident involving a federal inmate. The subsequent confidential report circulated among senior officials absolved the parole officers of any responsibility, noting that they had supervised Taylor as closely as possible. It pointed, instead, to the lack of treatment afforded the inmate both inside and outside the penitentiary.

The youth had received no treatment at Kingston Penitentiary, the report said, because of "the limited nature of programs suitable to this individual at the Regional Psychiatric Centre [the penitentiary's treatment facility] and the perception that there were many more desperate cases at KP."

With respect to the outside treatment resources available after Taylor's release, the inquiry noted: "All too often [the Correctional Service of Canada] appears to go begging hat in hand for facilities for our most difficult and needy class. . . . There exists a strong and effective resistance to accepting cases such as Taylor even on the part of provincially and federally funded treatment centres designed to administer to this type of case. Resistant as well are many of the community residential centres [halfway houses] under contract to the Correctional Service of Canada. Furthermore, there appears to be a very limited tolerance . . . to cases that are accepted. The inevitable result is we find discharges back on our doorstep shortly thereafter."

Nonetheless, the report said, efforts to obtain treatment for Taylor outside the prison might have been more successful if the prison psychiatrist and psychologist, along with the institution's case management team, had become involved in the search, rather than leaving it to one parole officer.

The inquiry concluded, among other things, that the federal government should expand the psychiatric treatment program within Kingston Penitentiary. It should establish liaison with the various other federal, provincial, and private agencies capable of providing treatment to such inmates. And notwithstanding the latter, it should "locate or establish a community resource with federal funding that will provide services to difficult [mandatory supervision] cases."

On August 28, 1981, Art Trono, Regional Director General of CSC in Kingston, dispatched the results of the inquiry to the commissioner of corrections in Ottawa. In a covering memorandum, Trono pledged: "We will spare no effort in once again endeavouring to improve our procedures with community and mental health officials."

In the intervening years, little has changed. Three years after April Morrison's murder, Marshall and his colleague Howard Barbaree were given a grant by CSC to initiate a treatment program at Kingston Penitentiary for sex offenders with subnormal intelligence. That program remains in effect today (although it is no longer administered by Marshall and Barbaree). However, many sex offenders still receive no treatment in federal penitentiaries in Canada. Most important, little effort is made to secure appropriate treatment for violent offenders released to the community. And the wrangling continues over who should pay for the treatment that is available outside the prison walls.

Indeed, seven years after the Taylor inquiry concluded, a coroner's jury investigating the brutal rape and murder of Tema Conter, a twenty-five year old fashion buyer for a Toronto boutique, urged the Canadian government to pay provincial health insurance premiums for all federal penitentiary inmates to enable offenders to obtain outside psychiatric treatment.

The recommendation followed an astonishing chain of events that saw the National Parole Board release a triple rapist and murderer from a medium-security penitentiary in eastern Ontario to a Toronto halfway house which parole officials knew was inadequately supervised. Even more bewildering is the fact that when it granted six forty-eight hour passes to Melvin Stanton in January 1988, the parole board was aware that over the previous six months, the thirty-one year old inmate of Warkworth Institution had trashed his cell, threatened to kill a prison worker, pulled a knife on another inmate, and been caught smoking marijuana. He had served seventeen years of an accumulated twenty-five year sentence and was twenty months away from being eligible for mandatory supervision.

Temporary absence passes are considered the first stage in an inmate's gradual release program. Typically, they range from escorted outings of several hours to unescorted excursions lasting twenty-four to seventy-two hours. They can usually be granted, at the parole board's discretion, after an offender has served one-sixth of his sentence.

Just three months before Stanton was let out on his first forty-eight-hour pass, he was sent to Kingston Penitentiary for a psychiatric assessment. Neil Conacher, the prison psychiatrist, wrote that the inmate was "angry and bitter and, despite what he says he thinks, obviously blaming the system for the way he feels. He is confused and uncertain underneath, obviously sincere in his distress. . . . There is a risk that he will decide that there is no hope, and staff must be alert for signs of suicidal planning." In his final report, Conacher said there was little that KP's treatment centre could do for Stanton and he strongly supported a graduated release plan for the inmate.

One month before Stanton was granted the pass, a Warkworth psychologist said the offender was "close to despair." Lynn Stewart recommended that he be granted full parole in order to attend a four-month treatment program for sex offenders at Toronto's Clarke Institute. "There is nothing more to be gained for Mr. Stanton by keeping him in prison," Stewart wrote in her assessment for the parole board. "Indeed, there is a high potential for self destruction, acting out and even suicide if he is detained. He requires a structured parole program for the next two years to prepare him for [eventual] independence."

As the coroner's jury would later hear, the plan to send Stanton to the Clarke Institute collapsed because the health services department at Warkworth did not have $7,000 to pay for the ten-day assessment. Pat Patterson, the department head, testified that the prison's budget for both physical and mental health care traditionally runs out halfway through each fiscal year.

Ontario, along with the other provincial governments, will provide health insurance to inmates granted full parole—their health care needs are considered the sole responsibility of the federal government while they are incarcerated—but the National Parole Board refused to give Stanton full parole. Douglas Crosbie, one of the parole board members present at the hearing, later told the inquiry that the proposal was rejected because it would have been impossible for the board to return the inmate to prison after treatment unless he violated the terms of his parole. Instead, in a move which Stanton's prison case management team later described as shocking, the board granted the inmate a series of six unescorted forty-eight-hour passes to Montgomery Centre in Toronto, a private halfway house under contract to CSC. The case workers said they had recommended that Stanton be given shorter escorted passes to the community.

A parole officer at Keele Centre, one of CSC's own halfway houses in Toronto, was blunt in his reaction six months earlier to Stanton's application for some form of release: "There can be no valid reason for this man to come to Toronto. [Metropolitan Toronto Police] protest him coming here in the strongest possible terms." Similarly, staff at Horizon House in Ottawa rejected Stanton, noting that the police force there did not want the offender released in its jurisdiction either, "especially since he isn't from Ottawa."

One of the National Parole Board's own members, Mac Stienberg, wrote in 1984, after denying Stanton day parole: "The violence in this case is alarming and must be a major concern when any review is undertaken. If ever he is to be considered for conditional release, there must be some very dramatic changes supported by an abundance of positive evidence of change. Unless such change takes place, or if there is not evidence of improvement, this man would have to be regarded as a dangerous release at [his mandatory supervision date in 1989]."

Stanton's erratic behaviour in prison was not the only cause for concern. A scant three months before the inmate's fateful hearing, Simonne Ferguson, the National Parole Board's Ontario director, told one of her staff in a letter that recent events had raised "serious questions regarding the quality of supervision" at Montgomery Centre. A resident of a nearby high-rise apartment building had notified police after seeing two inmates and two women partying on the roof of the halfway house. Another inmate, whose parole conditions strictly forbade him to leave the centre between

11:00 P.M. and 7:00 A.M., was given permission to leave at 5:30 A.M., and subsequently pushed a woman to the ground and stole her purse. A fourth inmate had been ordered out of the house, rather than being detained for correctional authorities, after he began ripping kitchen cupboards off the wall. Nonetheless, on January 13, 1988, with Ferguson present as an observer, a two-member parole board panel granted Stanton six unescorted passes to Montgomery Centre.

On January 25, thirty-six hours after he had arrived at the halfway house, Stanton escaped and attacked Tema Conter as she was walking out of her apartment on her way to work. He dragged her back into her home, knocked her unconscious, bound, gagged and raped her, and then stabbed her eleven times. He was arrested three days later while driving a stolen car near Wawa, Ontario, several hundred miles away.

The need for intense supervision of the inmate was apparently obvious to all but the parole board members, although they were well aware of Stanton's history. Just two weeks before he was released, one of his case workers noted in a report that the offender had grown up in prison, was "totally institutionalized" and had "only criminal values." One of the many psychiatrists and psychologists who assessed the inmate observed five years earlier that Stanton's prison-formed emotions and bitterness were "somewhat chilling."

Stanton's childhood in the oil fields of Alberta was marked by physical abuse, neglect and emotional deprivation. Although he was bright, his aggressive and impulsive behaviour led to problems with his teachers. He became a chronic truant and began stealing and taking drugs. When he was twelve years old, he was sent to a reform school. Years later, in a tearful interview with a psychologist at Kingston Penitentiary, he would recall how he had been sexually abused by the older juveniles at the school and, later, by older inmates in prison. He had raped women, he said, to get even.

When he was fourteen years old, Stanton was given a pass from Alberta Hospital in Edmonton, where he was receiving counselling to help him integrate with his family. After sniffing nail-polish remover, he walked into an apartment complex over a downtown business. When he was challenged by the caretaker's sixty-two year old wife, he grabbed the woman by the neck, punched her in the face, pulled her into a washroom and raped her. Four months later, before his scheduled appearance in juvenile court on that crime, he and his girlfriend were taking LSD in a park when he went berserk and beat her to death with a rock. He said she had accused him of being "queer."

On March 17, 1971, his fifteenth birthday, Stanton entered the federal penitentiary system; he had been sentenced to six years for manslaughter. A psychiatrist who assessed him at Drumheller Institution in Alberta told the National Parole Board there was still cause for hope. "This boy does not show a strong sense of hostility toward the world, but rather a sense of futility and indifference. . . . Since he is so young, I think there is still the possibility of growth and improvement in his character." However, this doctor expressed concern that the detrimental influence of a prison setting might limit his progress. "It would be advisable to have someone here take as much interest as possible in him. He has not had the experience of forming either deep or lasting relationships, and if he could feel that he was establishing some kind of rapport with those interested in him here, there is a distinct possibility that over a period of time his character could be moulded and changed to his and society's advantage."

Stanton's next psychiatric report would not be as optimistic. The next year, while he was being assessed at Alberta Hospital, he escaped and accumulated more charges, including break and enter and arson. He was caught and had five years added to his prison term. In a letter to probation officials on March 7, 1973, B.W.M. Dorran, director of the hospital's forensic unit, said the institution had no program that would benefit Stanton. Instead of behavioural therapy, Dorran suggested that the sixteen-year-old be lobotomized to control his aggression and impulsivity. He repeated his advice to the parole board a few months later. "With this type of personality, one would not expect a burning out process to begin until his early forties and, of course, there is the rare personality who never burns out until he is senile." Stanton told authorities it was discussions of brain surgery that had caused him to bolt from the hospital. Neurosurgery was never performed. However, according to the Kingston Penitentiary psychologist who interviewed him years later, "awareness of the appalling possibility served to intensify the problems of a [sixteen-year-old] boy."

When Stanton arrived at the penitentiary service's new regional psychiatric centre at Abbotsford, British Columbia, in the mid-1970s, he had spent most of the previous three years in prison heavily sedated and locked in solitary confinement. He complained that he had trouble sleeping, had frequent nightmares and could not control his temper. During his year-long stay there, he participated in individual and group psychotherapy, took courses to upgrade his education, and received biofeedback to reduce his level of anxiety and tension.

At the end of this program, Ali Saad, the penitentiary's psychiatrist, told the parole board that Stanton had improved. But, he added, "It is difficult to say whether this improvement will continue on the street or not and a period of probation or gradual access to society might be of help in getting him through the transition." Saad's prognosis: "Guarded."

Stanton was on day parole from a prison in Mission, British Columbia, in 1978, when he raped a second woman; he had another six years added to his sentence.

In 1979, he stole a pickup truck from the grounds of Riverview Psychiatric Hospital in Vancouver, where his sanity was once again being assessed, and escaped by driving the vehicle through a wire fence. Two hours later, he confronted a female janitor who was hauling garbage bags out of a school. He pushed the woman back into the building, threw her to the floor and took the keys to her car. When he made a motion as if to strike her, the woman pleaded with him not to hurt her because she was five months pregnant. Stanton ripped off her clothing and raped her before fleeing in her vehicle. He was caught by police early the next morning in Stanley Park.

The judge who sentenced Stanton in 1980 to eight years for this crime recommended that the habitual rapist spend part of his sentence in a provincial psychiatric hospital and return to such a hospital at the conclusion of his prison term. It was not to be.

From his 1980 conviction until his release in 1988, Stanton's time was divided between Kingston Penitentiary and Warkworth Institution, where he was sent to learn coping skills for community living. However, he did not receive any counselling at Warkworth; the staff reported that Stanton's attitude made it impossible to work with him. Testimony at an inquest into Tema Conter's death told a different story: Robert Cannon, one of only two psychologists dealing with almost five hundred inmates (including more than two hundred sex offenders) from 1985 to mid-1987, said he and his colleague were so busy writing reports for the parole board and responding to crises that they had no time to provide regular therapy.

As Stanton waited for the four months of treatment

that he would eventually receive at Kingston Penitentiary, his mood and his behaviour deteriorated. In February 1985, a prison guard reported to Stanton's case management team: "Stanton is becoming depressed and distressed. . . . If the problems bothering him are not looked into, it could present future problems for the inmate and the institution." A month later, Stanton smashed up his cell for the first time and threatened to commit suicide. A week after that, he was caught looking through a hall ventilator into a women's staff washroom. In August 1985, his case management team reported: "Stanton seems to suffer from bouts of depression where he feels that no one wants to do anything for him. He is extremely aggressive and exhibits explosive behavior."

The offender's spirits picked up the following January when he was informed that he would be transferred to KP for treatment in July. Stanton was reportedly well motivated during his four months of therapy, which included sex education and social skills training, and his case workers at Warkworth noted on his return that he had developed a better attitude. But they said he would need reinforcement to prevent him from sinking into despondency once again. "This is an individual who will require continued psychiatric treatment in the community. . . . Release planning is to be approached with caution."

A year later, in June 1987, the positive gains had slipped. "Mel has again decided that enough is enough," a case worker reported. "He is tired of waiting [to be granted temporary absence passes to be assessed at the Clarke Institute]. He now says he wants to forget his [passes and parole]. He will stay until [his mandatory supervision date] or [the end of his sentence]. My speaking to him on this date had no effect."

Shortly afterwards, Stanton proceeded on the path of self-destruction that would, ironically, result in his release. Psychiatric and psychological reports, prepared for the parole board during the last half of 1987 and entered as evidence at the Conter inquest, made it clear that prison professionals were uncomfortable with a suicidal inmate on their hands and pushed for his release. Ensuring public safety was apparently considered someone else's responsibility.

Like Duane Taylor—and many other habitual sex offenders who were given freedom without adequate preparation or support—Stanton is now back in prison serving a life sentence with no possibility of parole for twenty-five years.

These cases are not unique. In the eight years between the rape-murders of young April Morrison and Tema Conter, judges and coroner's juries across Canada repeatedly called on the federal government to do a better job of protecting the public from dangerous sex offenders.

In 1982, a coroner in Kootenay, British Columbia, said that all federal penitentiary inmates should remain in prison until they receive a positive psychiatric assessment, regardless of whether their terms are complete. Alan Askey made the recommendation after reviewing the events leading to the murder of eleven children by Clifford Olson. The notorious killer was released from British Columbia's Matsqui medium-security penitentiary on mandatory supervision five months before his first murder, after being in and out of prison for twenty-three years. His mandatory supervision had been revoked four times in the previous four years.

In 1986, a provincial court judge in Brandon, Manitoba, urged the federal government to give high priority to providing the best possible treatment for dangerous sex offenders—wherever it is found—and to research designed to improve such treatment. Judge A. F. James delivered the exhortation in his report of an inquest into a 1984 rampage in which Kenneth Steingard, a sex offender on mandatory supervision, killed four people. Steingard was a quiet, lonely gardener who was shunned by women for his widely known record of three sexual assaults and sought refuge in pornography. When his only female friend spurned his proposal of marriage, he became enraged and stabbed her to death. The following day, he shot his cousin's wife and her young son and daughter; before murdering the ten-year-old girl, he raped her. Two days later, after scribbling the details of the murders on scraps of paper, Steingard shot himself.

Judge James ruled: "The supervision accorded Steingard after his release in March 1983 was well-meaning but inadequate and, in the case of psychiatric supervision, totally inadequate, due not to neglect of duty to those involved, but rather to a heavy workload and lack of adequate resources available. It was, in effect, token supervision only."

In 1987, a coroner's jury in Ottawa, Ontario, said all federal penitentiary inmates should undergo in-depth psychological testing as soon as they arrive in prison, and the results should be used to develop appropriate rehabilitation programs. Before they are released, they should be reassessed, the jurors said. And if they are violent offenders, "a thorough, independent, psychiatric and psychological evaluation must take place at an outside psychiatric facility."

If psychiatric problems were identified at the time of the offence, "the parole release must include a special condition that the parolee will attend for professional counselling, psychiatric treatment and monitoring while on parole. In these cases, there should be periodic administration of psychological tests." This appeal followed an inquest into the killing of an Ottawa halfway house worker by Allan James Sweeney, a paroled murderer. The twenty-one-year-old woman was on duty alone at night, when she was ambushed in the basement, sexually assaulted, mutilated, and stabbed to death. Sweeney had committed an almost identical previous crime but had received no treatment inside or outside the penitentiary because prison officials were unaware that his first murder was a sex attack. They were also unaware, as revealed by psychiatric tests conducted at the Royal Ottawa Hospital after the second murder, that Sweeney was a sexual sadist who suffered from an antisocial personality disorder.

In the spring of 1988, an inquest jury in Burnaby, British Columbia, was singing the same tired refrain. The jury had probed the case of Allan George Foster, who was released from prison after serving seven years of a life sentence for raping and murdering his eighteen year old sister-in-law.

The thirty-seven year old cabinetmaker stayed out of trouble for the first five years of his parole. But by mid-1986, he was losing control. He was convicted of indecent exposure and returned to prison until the end of the year. Back on the street, Foster began drinking, smoking marijuana, and acting out his sexual fantasies, through obscene phone calls. He admitted his activities to his parole officers, but nothing was done. A year later, in December 1987, Foster bludgeoned his common-law wife to death with a hammer. He then killed her daughter and her daughter's friend, both of whom were twelve years old, and sexually assaulted their corpses. He turned himself in to police and, two weeks later, committed suicide by driving two ballpoint pens into his heart.

Foster attended a group program for sex offenders during his last year in the community, but the jury concluded that "the ongoing treatment of Foster's sexual addiction was seriously impaired by his use of a mind-altering substance. Dual therapy was imperative."

All sex killers should undergo combined therapy inside prison, the jury said, and the treatment should be continued when they are released. Outside therapy programs should be reviewed every three months, and paroled convicts should undergo mandatory tests for drug and alcohol use on the same basis. "At the present time, adequate therapy treatment programs do not exist in the community," the jury ruled. "We, therefore, recommend that such therapy programs be made available."

As the 1990s begin, the federal government has yet to make the treatment of sex offenders a priority either inside or outside the prison walls. It is not providing the money to treat every imprisoned rapist and pedophile; in fact, of the 1,400 sex offenders incarcerated in federal prisons, penitentiary treatment programs can accommodate fewer than two hundred a year. Neither is the federal government paying provincial health insurance premiums to allow federal inmates to obtain outside psychiatric and psychological treatment.

The lack of adequate treatment is just one aspect, however, of the criminal justice system's failure to deal with sex offenders.

2

Bureaucratic Bungling
and Indifference

WHEN THE INQUEST into Tema Conter's death ended
just before Christmas 1988, it was clear to Ross Bennett,
Ontario's chief coroner, what had gone wrong. For six
long weeks, penitentiary staff, National Parole Board
members, halfway house workers, and police officers
had attested to the events that led to the savage rape
and murder of the twenty-five-year-old Toronto fashion
buyer by a habitual sex offender on a two-day pass from
prison. Their testimony was often contradictory, but the
coroner was unequivocal in his conclusions: "This inquest showed that every single level screwed up."

As observers of the criminal justice system know, it
was not the first time and it won't be the last. The
inquest was a dramatic illustration of the rifts that exist
not only between prisons and the other elements of the
system, but among various staff within the penitentia-

ries themselves. Competing interests and limited resources pit one group against the other and evoke infighting, frustration, and indifference. A pass-the-buck mentality—driven in part by the political consequences of a mistake—is widespread and intensifies in the face of the failures it inevitably invites. With so many players, however, the responsibility is frequently spread thinly. Jane Pepino, a lawyer who headed the federal government's own internal inquiry into Tema Conter's death, commented afterwards: "Looking back, no one was to blame, but no one person was blameless."

Jurors at the Toronto inquest heard an incredible tale that began with the skewed values that led psychiatrists and psychologists to push for Melvin Stanton's release *because* he was despondent and potentially suicidal. A mixture of naiveté and arrogance caused parole board members to grant the inmate a series of unescorted passes, over a case worker's objections, without even discussing the fact that he had raped women on three previous occasions after either escaping or being temporarily released from custody. Expediency spurred prison officials to drop Stanton at the door of the privately run halfway house on short notice, without giving the staff adequate information about his record. Cynicism provoked the halfway house supervisor to go back to sleep after being informed in the middle of the night that the inmate had escaped. And apathy apparently led the Toronto police to wait more than eight hours for a photograph of the man before initiating a search for him.

A psychiatrist from Kingston Penitentiary testified that he recommended against more treatment for Stanton in the prison system because the inmate's rage was all he had: "If his anger started to fade, his inner core would fail. I suspected he would attempt suicide and probably be successful."

The supervisor of Montgomery Centre said he did

not personally contact correctional authorities when he first learned that Stanton was loose because of the "passive sabotage" he had experienced from penal and parole officials when he originally left the penitentiary service to help run the halfway house. The operation of the house had been turned over to a nonprofit organization under a privatization plan introduced by the Conservative government in 1986 and vehemently opposed by many correctional service employees. The director told the inquest that his relationship with his former colleagues had become almost competitive in nature. For example, he said, when he complained about prison inmates being dropped off without proper notice, he was told it was his problem. Another reason he did not act immediately, he said, was that he knew it would take police hours to organize a search.

Metropolitan Toronto Police took a passive role in dealing with Stanton's escape, a senior officer said, because the force had only sketchy information on the inmate. He had never lived in Toronto or been arrested there, and the police did not know what he looked like: "Where do you start looking for someone like that?"

For the chief coroner, it was all reminiscent of a 1987 Ottawa inquest over which he had also presided. In fact, Bennett said in his strongly worded charge to the Toronto jurors, if the recommendations of the previous inquest had been implemented, Tema Conter would still be alive.

The same gaping holes in the flow of communication among all facets of the criminal justice system—the same shifting of responsibility—had been uncovered a year earlier. And a comprehensive package of twenty-nine proposals had been carefully worked out to prevent a similar tragedy.

The Ottawa inquest, examining the circumstances surrounding the sex-murder of a halfway house worker by paroled killer Allan Sweeney, revealed that prison and parole officials did not know that Sweeney's original crime was sex-related when he entered the penitentiary system—or when he was released. Prison authorities waited five years before they requested details of the first murder from the investigating police force and the trial judge. And when they received only minimal information from the police and nothing from the judge, they did not pursue the issue. Instead, they relied primarily on the inmate's account of his offence, which he portrayed as no more than a break and enter gone awry.

Sweeney was initially sentenced to life in prison in 1975 at the age of nineteen, after he mutilated and stabbed to death a female neighbour while her two children slept. The sexual motive of the attack was clearly established at his trial, and a psychiatrist testified that "given similar circumstances, if such were possible, the same thing could happen again." The information was not conveyed to penitentiary officials, who later said that Sweeney was recommended for day parole after nine and a half years because he was a "model prisoner."

When the murderer was granted day parole in 1984, the coroner's jury was told that the Ottawa halfway house staff who accepted him were not even aware that Sweeney's first victim was a woman. The executive director of the local John Howard Society, which operates Kirkpatrick House, testified that inadequate information from correctional authorities about parolees was nothing new: "In the last fifteen years, it's been a constant source of discussion."

The lawyer representing the John Howard Society accused the Ottawa police force of abandoning responsibility for parolees to the parole board. He made the charge after asking a sergeant with the Ottawa force why no one in his department had telephoned police in Sault Ste. Marie, Ontario, for details of Sweeney's

original crime once it was known that Sweeney would
be on parole in their jurisdiction. The officer replied
that the information should have been supplied by the
parole board.

In 1985, when Sweeney was granted full parole
and allowed to leave the halfway house, testimony
revealed that his parole officers relied primarily on the
convict's girlfriend to report any violations of the terms
of his release. Yet, a year later, they ignored her
warning of impending disaster. In a terrified state, the
woman reported that Sweeney had been drinking and
taking drugs for months and that he had broken into
her home and stabbed a threatening note into her
kitchen table with a knife. The police did not lay
charges. And the parole officer did not inform the
parole board; later, the officer told the coroner's inquest
she did not think there were sufficient grounds for
suspending his parole. A manager of CSC's parole service
explained that her staff was inexperienced and "pushed
pretty much to the limit" supervising two hundred area
parolees. (Although the parole service ideally assigns
one parole officer to every twenty-five to thirty-five
offenders, in larger cities, officers can be responsible for
as many as sixty parolees each. Even with moderate
caseloads, officers are forced to rely primarily on contacts of the parolee to report whether he has broken the
terms of his release by, for example, drinking or taking
drugs. If the parole officers determine there is sufficient
evidence to recommend that an inmate's parole be
suspended, they have two weeks to prepare a report for
the parole board. According to internal memos of National Parole Board officials made public by liberal M.P.
John Nunziata, three inmates who allegedly violated
the terms of their parole in July 1987 were not referred
to the parole board because their parole officers missed
the fourteen-day deadline.)

Two weeks after he left the hate note, Sweeney's

drinking did result in a suspension of his parole. But
the parole board, still unaware of the threatening letter,
released him from jail after a month on the condition
that he return to Kirkpatrick House. Fifteen days later,
at one o'clock in the morning, the lone female staffer at
the house telephoned her supervisor to report that
Sweeney had returned late and was acting strange. It is
believed to be the last phone call she made before she
was raped, mutilated and stabbed to death. In sentencing Sweeney to life imprisonment with no parole for at
least twenty-five years, an Ontario Supreme Court Justice said it was "very difficult to find words adequately
to express the unspeakable inhumanity that was wrought."

When the public inquest into the Ottawa slaying
concluded, James Kelleher, Canada's solicitor-general
at the time, pledged that the federal government would
move quickly to improve the correctional system so that
the young halfway house worker would not have died in
vain. The government did not respond quickly enough.
In Toronto eight months later, Stanton's fourth rape
victim, Tema Conter, was dead.

The Ottawa jurors had recommended that parole
hearings be formally recorded; Stanton's hearing was
not. They suggested that all violent offenders undergo
an independent psychiatric examination prior to their
release; Stanton did not. They proposed that a careful
evaluation be done before releasing an inmate to a
halfway house to ensure that the facility is suitable;
Stanton was sent to Montgomery Centre despite the
fact that it was run by a fledgling organization and had
well-known security problems. The Ottawa jurors also
recommended that all halfway house staff be fully briefed
on new admissions prior to an inmate's arrival; clearly
that did not happen in Stanton's case.

Several weeks after Stanton was arrested, Kelleher
told Canadians that the protection of the public would
henceforth take priority over "the good of the offender"

when it came to releasing criminals from prison: "The overriding criteria has to be, will releasing him constitute undue risk to the public? That is now going to be the guiding principle."

When the inquest into the Conter murder concluded, Paul Evraire, the lawyer who had represented both the Correctional Service of Canada and the National Parole Board, said Perrin Beatty, Canada's acting solicitor-general, was anxiously awaiting the jury's recommendations and was committed to changing the system to avoid similar tragedies. Beatty told the House of Commons that all thirty-two reforms suggested by the Ottawa jury nineteen months earlier had been accepted by the government, but seven still had not been implemented because "of their complexity."

David Cole, the criminal lawyer who represented Toronto's Montgomery Centre, echoed the concern of many observers of the system when he said he feared the government's momentum would be short-lived. "My guess is that in six months, you'll see a great burst of programs and plans, and the new minister can attract some attention and look good. But my worry is that three years from now, they'll cut back again." (Professionals within the correctional service confirm that it is not uncommon for the government to earmark money for programming and then slowly divert it to other areas. In the mid-1980s, for example, the government approved funds to hire ten full-time staff to develop special programs and a separate range at Kingston Penitentiary for inmates whose emotional or mental handicaps made it impossible for them to integrate with the regular prison population. The extra money went initially to cover a short-fall in security and then disappeared; the special programs still do not exist.)

Ontario's outspoken chief coroner was even more cynical. "Something is missing in the correctional service organization," Bennett told the jurors. "The machinery is set up and the people are in place, but there is what could be described as a cavalier attitude." His remark was dismissed by Dennis Curtis, a government public relations officer, who termed it "incorrect and uncalled for." But a look at the criminal justice system's handling of other dangerous sex offenders across Canada in recent years—and the heavy toll it has exacted in human suffering—suggests otherwise.

In the summer of 1981, about the same time that Duane Taylor was walking out of Kingston Penitentiary, Paul Kocurek was released from Matsqui federal prison in British Columbia and returned to the vicinity of his hometown on Vancouver Island. He had served two-thirds of a two-year sentence for the indecent assault of a four year old girl—a crime he had committed one month after being placed on probation for unlawfully confining three young girls in his car.

At the first 1979 trial, a psychiatrist testified that Kocurek suffered from a schizophrenic illness and was obsessed with thoughts of sadomasochistic sexual encounters. Kocurek admitted that he was unable to reach orgasm unless he squeezed his girlfriend's neck, a practice the doctor warned could be dangerous. The judge put Kocurek on probation and recommended that he seek psychiatric help. Four weeks later, he was arrested again.

In sentencing Kocurek for the indecent assault, a county court judge concluded on the basis of more psychiatric reports: "This man is a very serious risk to the safety of children in the community." He said he was sentencing the offender to a federal penitentiary so that he could be treated. But Kocurek was deemed unsuitable for group therapy at the correctional service's regional psychiatric centre at Abbotsford, British Columbia, where he served part of his sentence, although he received some individual counselling there.

Six weeks after he was released on mandatory supervision, he struck again.

His last victim was a fifteen-year-old girl who was jogging along a quiet road at five o'clock on an August afternoon. Kocurek forced the girl into his car and raped her while tightening his hands around her throat until her heart stopped. Her body was found the next day buried under leaves in a remote wooded area about a mile from her home.

Testimony at his murder trial showed that Kocurek had not been properly supervised following his release from prison and, in fact, had been seen walking around the community with a starter's pistol and a pair of handcuffs, devices he apparently used in his fatal attack.

The *Vancouver Sun*, quoting unidentified sources, reported that a prison psychiatrist had warned that Kocurek would kill if he went untreated. The newspaper also revealed that the parole board warned local mental-health officials that the inmate should be closely monitored. Yet, when he failed to show up for his first appointment with them, no one bothered to inform his parole officer. An editorial called Kocurek "a classic example of a dangerous sex offender, a human time bomb the system failed to defuse."

Responding to a question about the case in the House of Commons in June 1982, Robert Kaplan, the solicitor-general of the day, said he planned to change the legislation regarding mandatory supervision. The law had been introduced in 1970 to require prisoners serving the last third of their sentences in the community to report to parole officers. Before then, they had been under no surveillance at all. But the parole board still could not delay the release of inmates it judged to be dangerous; if their behaviour in the institution was good, they had to be let out.

Kaplan was under intense pressure from the public and police and lawyers' groups. The outcry reached a peak when it was revealed that Clifford Olson had been freed on mandatory supervision in June 1980, five months before he killed the first of eleven children. Olson's complete sentence had actually expired by the time he began his rampage, but that was merely a technicality in the minds of the forces calling on the government to keep violent offenders in prison. Their demands were fuelled by widespread publicity of four additional murders in 1981 by inmates who were still on mandatory supervision. In addition to the children slain by Duane Taylor and Paul Kocurek, two women in Toronto were killed in separate incidents by men fresh out of prison.

As the public clamoured for the government to keep dangerous prisoners locked up for their entire sentences, Kaplan was being pressured in the opposite direction by the penal system. Penitentiaries were bursting at the seams. A nation-wide construction program had been delayed a year earlier, and a government restraint program had cut back on staff. Disturbances were erupting in prisons across the country; the most infamous of these was a bloody riot at Archambault, in Quebec, in which three guards were killed. Grievances from staff and prisoners soared. "Once more, the service was forced to scramble to acquire additional space and speed inmates through the system," an advisory committee to the solicitor-general later reported.

In early 1983, Terrence Keeler, a sex offender with two violent rapes on his record, was freed on mandatory supervision in Calgary, Alberta. Nine years earlier, Keeler had sexually assaulted his sister-in-law in a garage while holding a tent peg to her throat. He was on a weekend pass from his prison sentence for that crime when he raped a friend's wife at knife-point in her home.

Eight months after Keeler was released, he talked a twenty-eight-year-old woman, who was working alone

in a community hall, into letting him inside to buy a
club membership. He robbed the woman of $420,
raped her and then stabbed her numerous times with a
jackknife. He returned while she was attempting to
phone for help and stabbed her again before finally
leaving. Fortunately, she survived. Before he was caught,
Keeler tried to sexually assault a young mother at
knife-point in her home, but ran off when she grabbed
the weapon from him.

In July 1984, prison unrest flared again as 720
inmates across the country were doubled up in cells six
feet long and nine feet wide. The number of murders
among prisoners had more than doubled, from six in
1982-1983 to fourteen in 1983-1984; another thirty-two
inmates committed suicide over the two-year period.
An uprising at Stony Mountain Penitentiary in Manitoba
claimed the lives of two more guards. The guards'
union threatened to hold an illegal strike to protest
prison conditions; demonstrators outside Stony Mountain called for the return of the death penalty.

The same month, two adults and two children in
Brandon, Manitoba, were killed by Kenneth Steingard,
a sex offender on mandatory supervision, who then shot
himself.

A month later, in Edmonton, Alberta, Robert Fletcher, another offender serving the last third of his sentence in the community, abducted a sixteen year old
girl as she walked along a street at dawn. Fletcher
drove the teenager to a secluded field east of the city,
tore off her clothes and tied her to a tree. He sexually
assaulted her and stabbed her fourteen times in the neck
and chest before walking away. The victim managed to
free herself and crawl to a highway where she was
found by a passing motorist.

In the fall of 1984, the Progressive Conservative
Party took power in Ottawa. And the following summer,
Solicitor-General Elmer McKay proposed the legisla-

tive change that would enable the parole board to prevent the automatic release of potentially violent prisoners who had served two-thirds of their sentences. Critics charged that the proposal was a Band-Aid solution for serious problems within the entire penal-parole system—a far cry from the comprehensive and fundamental changes recommended by myriad inquests and inquiries. Time would prove them right.

There were at least two more sexually motivated murders in Canada before the law did change. In July 1985, Sweeney murdered the Ottawa halfway house worker. The same month, Bruce John James, a sex offender on mandatory supervision in British Columbia, fatally beat a woman while attempting to sexually assault her. She died in hospital thirteen days after she was discovered nude and semi-conscious in a rural subdivision north of Nanaimo.

In August 1986, the parole board finally got the power to detain dangerous inmates past their mandatory supervision dates. Critics who were not familiar with the system were placated; those who were, viewed the change with disdain. It was, in the words of Graham Stewart, director of reform for the John Howard Society on Ontario, a "fool's paradise." Indeed, subsequent events have shown that a mere legislative amendment could not protect the public from violent offenders. The parole board has proved it has no better than random luck in predicting which inmates will reoffend, although it has occasionally gone to extreme lengths to improve its record. In early 1988, parole board members in British Columbia were reported to have resorted to handwriting analyses to determine whether certain prisoners should be released.

In June 1987, a year after the parole board's mandate was strengthened, the public was again demanding that the government take action to reform the system.

The board had granted Daniel Gingras, a convicted

murderer, a day pass from a maximum-security penitentiary in Alberta to visit the West Edmonton Mall for his thirty-sixth birthday. Gingras escaped from his escort and, six weeks later, he abducted a twenty-four-year-old upholstery shop seamstress who was getting into her pickup truck in a shopping mall parking lot in Medicine Hat, Alberta. He needed a getaway vehicle for a robbery he had planned. When the woman started "whining," he strangled her with her own shoelaces and dumped her body into a ditch twelve miles south of the city. Two days after that, he robbed and shot to death an Edmonton drifter. He was sentenced to life in prison with no chance of parole for twenty-five years.

The correctional service ordered an internal investigation into the incident and later, in the face of political pressure, commissioned John Weir, an Edmonton lawyer, to conduct a second, independent inquiry, which lasted five months. Weir found that the parole board had been given inadequate information on which to base a decision but concluded, "It may well be, with more experience, parole board members might have been less trusting of the assertions of [penitentiary] case management [workers] where there was a prisoner with the background of Gingras."

In October 1987, the board released another convicted killer, Bruce Bird, on mandatory supervision in British Columbia, after determining that he was not a dangerous offender. A month later, Bird broke into a middle-aged couple's home at midnight. He sexually assaulted and terrorized them for three hours before tying them up and fleeing in their car. He had twelve years added to his prison term.

In March 1988—three months after its ill-fated decision to give Melvin Stanton a series of passes—the parole board freed Joseph Fredericks from an Ontario prison where he had served two-thirds of a five-year sentence for sexually assaulting a boy in Ottawa. Three

months afterwards, Fredericks kidnapped an eleven
year old boy at a shopping mall in Brampton, Ontario,
and repeatedly raped him before stabbing him to death.
Fredericks, too, was sentenced to life in prison with no
possibility of parole for twenty-five years. Parole officers
testified at his trial that they were unaware, among
other things, of his long history of sexually assaulting
children "because of the quickness of his release."
Ontario's chief coroner called another inquest. (The
fees at the Stanton inquest for jurors, independent
witnesses and court reporters alone totalled $13,000.
Taxpayers ultimately also paid the larger but uncalculated
costs associated with the salaries and expenses of the
chief coroner, crown counsel and lawyers, and of the
correctional service employees who testified.)

In November 1988, a thirty-year-old Edmonton
man, released on mandatory supervision after serving
two-thirds of a five-year sentence for indecent assault,
was charged with sexual assault and attempted murder
after a teenage girl was found lying unconscious at the
side of a road on the outskirts of the city.

The list goes on and on. The point is not that most
inmates released from prison commit violent crimes;
the majority do not. But the parole board cannot accurately predict who will. Its members are patronage
appointees, the majority of whom—53.3 percent according to a 1988 parliamentary committee report—have
no background in the criminal justice system. (In early
1990, there were thirty full-time members, who were
each paid between $75,000 and $88,000 a year; fifty-six
part-time members, who received a per diem fee that
ranged from $375 to $440; and forty-nine community
members, who earned $200 a day. The community
members are involved only in parole hearings for offenders
serving indeterminate or life sentences; two community
members join two regular members at these hearings.)

In determining when inmates should be released

from prison, the members rely partially on the recommendations of prison and parole staff and largely on their gut instincts. A witness at the 1988 hearings of a House of Commons committee examining sentencing and parole, held in camera, complained that some parole board members feel they are "anointed rather than appointed."

Graham Stewart sees it this way: "The parole board gives parole to people who look like their sons. That's why guys like Stanton and Fredericks could get out, because they don't look like scary guys. The inmate who walks into a parole hearing with 'Fuck Cops' tattooed on his forehead doesn't get out regardless of his crime. He could be a bicycle thief.

"It's human nature to want to forgive people who are remorseful. If we can be convinced that they are remorseful, we tend to want to relieve them of some of the burden of their punishment. It's not a bad thing. It's part of a healthy personality; but it's not a good predictor.

"These guys can feel enormous guilt. They can feel enormous responsibility. They can be highly motivated to change. But they can still have a compulsion that they can't control. Let's grow up and realize what we are talking about here."

A sex offender's record in prison is no indication of future behaviour either. After all, there are few women and no children inside men's penitentiaries. "There is a certain arrogance and naiveté on the part of the parole board," says a prison bureaucrat. "They think if a person is neat and clean in jail, he will do well on the street. And if they can establish a rapport with an inmate, they think they will have a positive impact on him."

Even if the parole board could predict which inmates will be violent, it is only postponing the inevitable by detaining them. With very few exceptions, even dangerous offenders will eventually get out: the parole board reports that 90 percent of all federal inmates return to the community within seven years even without parole. The existence of parole and mandatory supervision not only gives inmates something to work towards while they are behind bars, it allows correctional authorities to control their reintroduction into society. Once an offender's sentence has expired, parole officials have no authority to exercise any control on his activities. In explaining why he supports gradual release programs that allow inmates to be reintegrated slowly into society, David Cole, the Toronto criminal lawyer, says: "Hey, I don't want some guy coming out of the hole at Millhaven [maximum-security penitentiary in Ontario] on the last day of his sentence and sitting beside me on the bus the next morning."

The logic behind the gradual release of inmates is clear. The catch is—as a federal government task force headed by Erik Nielsen reported in 1986—there is "discouragingly little" in the form of meaningful programs for offenders on either side of the fence. And the parole board could not insist that parolees participate in such programs even if they did exist.

"The only authority the parole board has is to release people or not release people," says Stewart. "They don't have any control over treatment—over ensuring that there really is some rehabilitation going on. So, what they are really doing is avoiding sensationalism." Or trying to.

As the Melvin Stanton case illustrates, case management workers and psychologists do not always agree on whether or how an inmate should be released. But ignoring their recommendations can be perilous.

In late 1986, the parole board rejected case workers' suggestions that Douglas Barnes, who had two convictions for rape and one for indecent assault, be placed in a halfway house when he was released on mandatory supervision. The inmate had been tested by staff running the sex offender treatment program at Kingston Penitentiary, had been found not to have deviant sexual preferences and had been judged, therefore, not to need treatment. The board determined that the supervision of a parole officer was all that was necessary and sent Barnes back to his hometown east of Toronto.

Peter Longarini, the parole officer who assessed Barnes before his release from prison, said the inmate was bright, good-looking and charismatic: "The kind of guy that women would pick up in a singles' bar." And his behaviour in prison had been exemplary. Nonetheless, the fact that he refused to admit any responsibility for his crimes made Longarini and the other members of the case management team apprehensive: "We felt he needed more than just a parole officer supervising him, especially in an urban area where our resources are taxed. At least if he were in a halfway house, he would have to sleep there."

Despite the inability of parole officers in large urban centres to closely supervise inmates in the community, the parole board opted not to release Barnes to a halfway house. Eleven months after his release, he raped a twenty-three-year-old woman at knife-point in the parking lot of a community college where he was taking a welding course.

It is far from certain that the outcome would have been altered simply by sending Barnes to a halfway house (there are thirteen houses operated by CSC and 149 funded by the government and run by a non-profit agency—such as the Salvation Army—or, in one case, a private entrepreneur). There have been many failures.

In 1986, the parole board released Ross Evans, a rapist, from Kingston Penitentiary to a government-operated halfway house in Toronto, after determining he was not dangerous, but with a recommendation that he obtain psychiatric treatment. When Evans arrived at the centre, he was told that the correctional service did not have the resources to provide him with therapy; he would have to wait. Four days later, Evans broke into a Scarborough home and raped a thirty-year-old mother at knifepoint, after threatening to kill her and her baby. He has since been declared a dangerous offender and has been imprisoned indefinitely.

A year earlier, Lonnie Mowers, a paroled sex offender, walked away from Montgomery Centre, the same privately run halfway house from which Stanton escaped, and attacked five women in the Toronto area. In the last incident, Mowers talked three teenage girls he met at a hamburger shop into giving him a ride. He pulled a fake gun on them, made them drive to a secluded area and sexually assaulted them over a period of seventeen hours. He, too, was later declared a dangerous offender. (The parole board reviews each dangerous offender case after the first three years and then, if parole is denied, every two years afterwards. Like inmates serving life sentences, dangerous offenders granted parole remain under some form of supervision in the community unless the designation is quashed by a court, which has sole authority to do so.)

The parole officers assigned to supervise inmates in the community are often so overworked that they have lost track of inmates altogether. In 1989, for example, a sex offender paroled in Manitoba sexually assaulted three eight-year-old girls in Ontario after a "bureaucratic error" caused the parole officer to lose sight of the man; officials said they did not even know he had left the province.

In 1986, a parolee in Vancouver who had pleaded guilty to two violent sexual assaults and a string of bank holdups, told a provincial court judge that he had warned his parole officer that he was back on drugs, but nothing was done about it. "I was left to fight this battle alone," said Merek David Michaels before he was sentenced to another fifteen years in prison.

The duties of a parole officer have changed dramatically, Peter Longarini says, since he started supervising inmates in Hamilton, Ontario, in the early 1970s. Then, he spent a lot of time on the street, checking out the haunting grounds of the parolees in his charge: "There is an expression, 'standing six,' which means that one person stands watch for the others. When I was out, they had to have someone standing six all the time. It's the only way that you can have some effect. The only way that you can show them that you care—that it matters whether or not they drink, whether or not they hang around with people they are not supposed to. But they don't do parole like that now. The job has turned into a paper war." The parole board demands more detailed reports now for parole officers involved in case management. And whereas most officers were required in the past to assess the feasibility of only one release plan per inmate, they must now routinely check out several plans. Officers complain that a lot of the paper work is redundant and that the parole board does not have time to read it all anyway; across Canada, the board reviews an average of 375 files a month, of which 150 involve panel hearings.

With the cracks in the system virtually ensuring the failure of certain inmates, paper trails have become a necessity for correctional service workers who want to protect their jobs. "The parole board never admits it is wrong," said one employee. "It didn't even admit it was wrong with Stanton. The consequences of an error are always laid at the feet of an individual staffer. Whatever happens, you must protect the minister [the solicitor-general]."

Although the parole board has to approve day passes for convicted murderers, for example, it was the warden of the Alberta penitentiary that released Daniel

Gingras who bore the brunt of public outrage about the birthday pass. Shortly after the incident, the administrator was transferred to "non-operational duties."

In 1984, following a public uproar about four-time sex killer Wayne Boden walking away from his escort during lunch at a fashionable Montreal restaurant, Robert Kaplan responded that the prison officials responsible would be disciplined and perhaps fired.

Penitentiary employees are well aware that the arm's length relationship that is supposed to exist between politicians and the public service is not always upheld in the correctional service. Despite the long chain of command between the individual staff member and the minister—the unit manager, deputy warden, warden, deputy commissioner, and, finally, commissioner of penitentiaries—when a contentious issue arises, it is not unheard of for an underling to be called directly by staff in the minister's office.

Participating in a paper war may be expedient for career-minded workers involved in the penal-parole system, but it will do little to solve the gaps in communication. In the summer of 1988, for instance, the warden at Bowden Institution in Alberta gave approval for a sex offender at the prison to visit a hospital, providing he was escorted in leg-irons and handcuffs. The staff misinterpreted the pass to be a rehabilitation temporary absence, which does not require an inmate to be shackled. On the way back to Bowden, the two escorts and the inmate, James Fowler, stopped at a fast-food restaurant for a meal. When the threesome had finished their hamburgers, Fowler went back to the counter to buy an ice-cream cone. As the two guards sat discussing where to return their trays, the offender walked out the door. Before he was arrested, he had broken into five homes in Edmonton and sexually assaulted a fifty-five-year-old woman at gunpoint.

The same year, a parolee in Halifax, Nova Scotia,

robbed and killed a fifty-three-year-old woman four days after his mother telephoned police to report that he might be in possession of a stolen car. The police said they could not track down the man initially because his name was misspelled in the central computer. When they did find his name, he was listed as having been imprisoned for another crime and out on parole in British Columbia.

Around the same time, police in Montreal freed a suspected rapist as a result of another clerical error. The man, described in the subsequent Canada-wide warrant as dangerous, was awaiting arraignment on charges stemming from a break-in at a city home in which a sixteen-year-old girl had been raped. When an officer discovered that the man had two outstanding impaired driving charges against him, he was taken to provincial court to be tried on those first. He was found guilty and ordered to pay a fine. But then, because the forms accompanying him were not stamped to indicate he should be kept in custody, he simply walked away.

In 1983 in Calgary, the parole board misread an appeal court ruling that quashed a three-time rapist's dangerous offender status on his first conviction of sexual assault, but upheld it on the others. The board released the inmate and, four months later, he attacked his fourth victim.

Such bungling probably can never be totally eradicated, but it might be viewed in a more sympathetic light if it did not appear to stem from a callous indifference that springs from the federal government and trickles down through the entire criminal justice system.

The John Howard Society has called on the government to scrap the parole system as it now exists and replace it with a statutory gradual release system that would begin after two-thirds of every sentence. Rather than guessing which inmates should be let out, the parole board would instead spend its time determining the circumstances that should surround each release. In other words, it would concentrate on reducing the potential for future violence, not merely attempt to predict it. Under the plan, the most serious offenders would receive the most intense supervision and treatment. In rare situations, where an inmate's mental health made any release dangerous, the person would be transferred to a psychiatric institution.

The program will not work, of course, unless there is an honest commitment on the part of the government to eliminate the rifts and vastly improve the flow of communication among all segments of the criminal justice system. It must also provide secure halfway houses, sufficient parole officers to adequately supervise inmates in the community, and appropriate treatment and programs for discharged offenders. This is a massive task that will require far more than political posturing and fancy mission statements designed to improve public relations. Until the support is in place, dedicated workers in the various facets of the system will be forced to continue to do their best and then cross their fingers.

In the summer of 1989, as police in Ottawa searched for the pervert who sodomized and strangled a two-and-a-half year old boy and then threw his body into a dumpster across the street from his home, a bureaucrat with the federal correctional service was understandably apprehensive. "I just hope it isn't one of ours," he confided.

3

Behind the Walls

THE YOUNG MALE guard peering out a small barred opening in the door to E Block inside Kingston Penitentiary is obviously perplexed. "You want to what? Tour the range?" he says in an incredulous tone to two visitors standing in the hallway outside. "Holy cow, why?"

E Block is home to some of the worst criminals in Canada. Here, Melvin Stanton, Clifford Olson and thirty-one other men spend twenty-three hours a day locked inside cells smaller than the average Canadian bathroom. Loathed by even the regular inmates of the 155-year-old prison, who are themselves at the bottom of the hierarchy in the federal penal system, the residents are in what is known as protective custody within protective custody. In addition to child murderers and sex offenders, the range holds informants and other criminals who, for a variety of reasons, are also at risk of being killed in the general penitentiary population. They are allowed outdoors once a day from 8:00 A.M. until 9:00 A.M. when the exercise yard is empty of other inmates. They walk en masse to the kitchen to pick up their meals, when the rest of the prison is locked up, but return to their cells to eat. Every second day, they are permitted to shower in one of the two empty cells in their area outfitted for the purpose.

The bemused guard pulls open the massive door and gestures for the interlopers to enter. The polished linoleum on the floor in the outside foyer abruptly gives way to worn paint on concrete. The clanging and chattering is replaced by silence. Along the right-hand side of the rectangular range are two levels of cells, each barely large enough to hold a bed, a sink, a toilet, and a metal desk. An open staircase and a catwalk provide access to the top tier. Opposite, sunshine pours through windows high atop a two-tone brown and white block wall; at its foot, an automatic washer and dryer and a cleaning cart sit in front of open pipes. Two large white industrial fans mounted in the ceiling slowly circulate the air. At the far end of the enclosure, guards sit inside glassed-in rooms on both the top and bottom floors. The inmates have asked for traps to kill the rats they say scuttle through their cells at night and for wire mesh to keep out birds and squirrels.

At an inquest in late 1989 into the suicide the previous year of a sex offender in E Block, Clifford Olson described the segregation unit as "an inhumane form of torture." Not everyone would agree with his assessment, but no one argues that the range promotes the rehabilitation of its residents. It has not even the guise of treatment or programming. Nonetheless, Olson is the only one of the inmates there who wants to move into the general prison population. The others, while fighting for better conditions, want to stay right where they are and are fearful of a recent move by the correctional service to cut back the number of offenders in protective custody.

Silently, the guard leads the tour past the thirty-four cells, thirty-three of which are occupied. Inside one, a middle-aged man with a shock of white hair is writing at his desk, his large frame barely accommodated by the available space. In another, an inmate stands staring straight ahead at a bare wall. On the top floor, Olson is listening to music through headphones. Two cells down, Melvin Stanton is lying on his bed. He looks up as the visitors walk by, as if surprised to see anyone, but says nothing. Although it is just past noon, most of the inmates are sleeping. The empty blue plastic lunch trays protruding from the bars of their cells are the only sign that they have been awake at all that day.

It is normally quiet in E Block, the guard comments before showing the visitors out. Most of the inmates just want to be left alone. Even during the daily one-hour "recreational" period, the majority remain in their cells. "Best thing they ever did was to bring in cable television," he says. "They get it at a group rate."

Despite the television sets, it is easy to imagine, after touring E Block, what is must have been like at the prison 155 years ago, when Canada's "lunatic criminals" were housed in what the Board of Inspectors of the day called "underground apartments." These were small windowless cubicles in the subterranean part of the original building on the level of the sewer emptying into Lake Ontario. When a southwesterly wind created high tides, the dungeon flooded. It is not hard to picture, either, the inmate orderlies who, a mere twenty-five years ago, are said to have used knuckle dusters to deal with mental illness in the psychiatric ward that has since evolved into the penitentiary's Regional Treatment Centre.

"One of the staff was digging around the attic the other day," says Bill Miles, the senior psychologist at the treatment centre, as he escorts a visitor through the prison complex. "And he found the little black box that they used to give electroshock therapy." While the treatment of offenders has changed drastically over the years, the attitudes of some penitentiary staff have not kept pace.

The eighty-bed treatment centre lies along the northern perimeter of the twenty-three-foot wall that surrounds the Kingston Penitentiary complex. The centre consists of two century-old limestone blockhouses abutting a 1950s white stucco building that looks like an army barracks. Inside the front door, a guard peers suspiciously at a visitor. "Are you in psychology too?" he enquires, a hint of sarcasm in his voice.

The guard's remark epitomizes the rift that exists throughout the penitentiary service between the staff who believe in the potential for rehabilitating inmates and those who think that programs of any sort jeopardize security and, furthermore, are a waste of time and money because offenders either can't or won't change.

In this climate, none of the full-time psychologists at the treatment centre—five of whom work with sex offenders—has it easy. With meagre resources and little moral support, they are assessing and treating some of the most disturbed and reviled criminals in Canada. But perhaps the toughest job of all falls to Bruce Malcolm. The thirty-seven-year-old behavioural analyst has the unenviable task of deciding which of the sex offenders should be treated. The centre tries to assess every known rapist and pedophile incarcerated in federal prisons in Ontario and the Atlantic Provinces; however, it does not have the resources to treat them all. Of approximately 120 offenders a year who go through the centre's two-week assessment regimen, no more than 60 can be accommodated in its sixteen-week treatment program. And there is a waiting list: inmates wait, on average, a year to be tested and, if chosen, two years to be treated.

Until recently, Malcolm relied primarily on the results of high-tech physiological testing and his own intuition to determine which of the sex offenders assessed at the treatment centre should be added to the treatment schedule. Now, he asks the psychologists, who would eventually treat the inmate, and the nurses working with the prisoners on the ranges to participate in the decision-making process.

Sitting in his second-floor office that looks out onto the prison wall, the personable red-headed professional is candid. He does not want total responsibility for exempting a sex offender from treatment: "I don't have any problems in identifying someone as needing treatment. I wanted someone else's opinion on the guys I say I don't think need treatment, especially the guys that are iffy."

The decision is not always difficult, he says. Recently, for example, a sixty-five-year-old man was referred to the treatment centre for evaluation. He had been convicted and imprisoned on incest charges two decades after he had sexually assaulted his teenage daughters. In the intervening years, he had been offence-free. "We can't assume that a man who hasn't harmed anyone for twenty years still has a problem." Conversely, Malcolm says, there are offenders who are clearly in need of therapy. In between are the cases he wrestles with.

After reviewing the records of some offenders, he reasons, "If he committed that crime, there was something wrong. . . . But then we have the dilemma of CSC not providing the resources to treat everyone."

Malcolm is aware that identifying more offenders

than there are spaces in the treatment program will "create some very angry men, who have to sit in.prison for a long time and won't get treated." When they are eventually released, he says, "I'm not sure that they are any less dangerous. . . . The difference is that the Correctional Service of Canada is no longer responsible; they have complied with the law and kept them in for as long as they could possibly keep them. But they haven't served the public by trying to rehabilitate, or reduce the dangerousness of, those people.

"In all the time I've worked here, no one has ever come to me and said, 'You have to slow down the number of people that you recommend for treatment'; no one has ever even made a hint at that. [But] there is this overriding feeling that if I recommend everyone— and that covers my ass very conveniently—some of them won't get treatment and I may be creating more problems than I am solving."

Each sex offender assessed at the treatment centre undergoes an average of three hour-long tests in the laboratory across the hall from Malcolm's office. The door opens onto a control room lined from floor to ceiling with electronic equipment—tapes, cassette players, slide projectors, television monitors and a powerful engineering computer that crunches pages and pages of numbers into individual profiles of the offenders' sexual proclivities. Behind the far wall are three identical rooms. Each is painted dark slate blue. A vinyl reclining chair sits in front of a projection screen and a video camera. On the chair are two blue terry-cloth towels, earphones, and a small silicon ring with wires that trail up from a battery pack on the floor and out through a small opening in the wall to the computer outside.

A technician ushers one offender into each room, issues preliminary instructions, dims the lights, and leaves. From his command post outside their doors, he tells them through an intercom to place the silicon rings over their penises and to put on the earphones. What the offenders hear and see during the next hour or so depends on their crimes: the tests are individualized. Typically, though, they listen first to eight two-minute audio tapes, which graphically describe different consenting and nonconsenting sexual scenes. ("You are alone with a beautiful girl you met at a party. You can tell she is very attracted to you, and you would like to get to know her better. You move closer to her on the couch and kiss her. . . .") The scenarios are written by the psychology staff and are recorded by a skilled announcer.

The computer technology used in the laboratory was developed by doctors performing microsurgery to determine whether blood was flowing through severed fingers they had reattached; it is exceptionally sensitive. The flexible gauge around the inmate's penis contains a thin column of mercury through which a weak electrical current passes. As the man becomes aroused, the circle stretches and the mercury coil elongates, placing resistance on the current. The computer measures the voltage three times every second.

When the audio tapes are over, the offenders see a series of slides of males and females ranging in age from five to twenty-five. Each is pictured naked and alone. During this segment, the technician switches on the video cameras, which are trained on each man's face, and scans the monitors to ensure they do not try to foil the test by looking away from the screen. Again, the computer fastidiously records their responses.

The slides determine which gender and age group is most attractive to the men. The tapes assess their arousal to forced or violent sex. The amount of force varies. "The highest is a very brutal assault in which the guy punches the girl and there is blood flowing from her face," says Malcolm. "If a man becomes sexually aroused to that, there is very little doubt in our minds that he has a problem." The computer takes about an hour to analyse their reactions and translate them into curves on graph paper. In the meantime, the inmates answer "always, usually, sometimes, seldom or never" to a series of written questionnaires. ("Do women generally get what they deserve? If someone hits you, are you likely to hit them back? At a social event, do you stand in the corner and only talk to people who approach you?") Illiterate inmates have the questions read to them.

The physiological, or phallometric, tests are not infallible. The technician can tell if an inmate tries to manipulate the gauge—the voltage increases too quickly or falls off too suddenly. And, during the slide show, the video cameras eliminate the most obvious fakery. But, says Malcolm, smart inmates will cheat in another way. They will look at the picture but concentrate on the girl's hair or the rock behind her or the tree beside her. Even if a sex offender is not deliberately trying to confound the tester, the sterile environment of the laboratory may inhibit his deviant inclinations. Research at Kingston Penitentiary has shown that only fifteen percent of rapists and forty percent of child molesters demonstrate deviant preferences in this setting.

All the more reason for Malcolm to solicit other help in making his decision. He also carefully reviews the offender's history and record. If he is still unsure, he may deliberately provoke inmates. "Sometimes I try to make them angry to see how they will respond. I might tell them they need treatment just as a test." If they explode, they probably do.

Whatever his verdict, Malcolm insists on explaining it in person. "Some people say I'm crazy, but I won't let anyone leave here without telling him my opinion. If they don't like it, that's fine. But they are adults, serving a sentence in a federal prison. I refuse to write something on a piece of paper that I won't say to them."

Presented with Malcolm's edict, the offenders' reactions run the gamut. Of the two-thirds he determines to be in need of treatment, he says about five percent are grateful that they are finally going to get the help they need. At the other end of the spectrum, fifteen to twenty percent are outraged: "They get mad. I don't mean angry, I mean mad—fuming mad. They rant and rave. They question whether what we are doing is proper. They say the tests are lying or I am lying. They say we've got their results mixed up with someone else. They question my parentage." As for those he judges not in need of treatment, he quips, "They send me Christmas cards."

What most of the recalcitrant inmates often object to, Malcolm explains in a more serious vein, is not treatment per se, but the fact that the waiting lists for therapy mean they will have to serve longer sentences than they might otherwise. Because of the prison's strained resources, they cannot be accepted into a treatment program until long past their parole dates (after one-third of their sentences).

"If, as they walked in the door, we assessed them and said OK, you need treatment, and they immediately went into a treatment program, most of them would accept that. . . . Especially if at the end of the treatment program they were given an opportunity for release. But that is not the way the system works. We assess them at one-sixth of their sentences [when they are eligible for day parole]. Then, if they are identified as needing treatment, they go on a waiting list. That sees them treated at somewhere between one-half and two-thirds of their sentences [their mandatory supervision dates]."

Until mid-1989, only three correctional services institutions—in Kingston, Saskatoon and Abbotsford—offered treatment programs for sex offenders. In the wake of the publicity following the murder of Tema

Conter, the federal government asked Bill Marshall and Howard Barbaree, codirectors of the Kingston Sexual Behaviour Clinic, to establish another program at Warkworth medium-security penitentiary in eastern Ontario. More than eighty percent of the sex offenders incarcerated in federal prisons in Ontario are at KP or Warkworth, where they make up roughly half of the prison populations. Along with Beaver Creek minimum-security institution in the Muskokas in northern Ontario, the three institutions form a major subsystem in which sex offenders, who are at the very bottom of the prison pecking order, are relatively safe from the "solid cons."

The government's decision to establish a fourth treatment program also came on the heels of a lawsuit launched by thirteen sex offenders—ten at Warkworth and three at KP—asking the federal court to order the correctional service to provide inmates with the treatment that had been recommended for them and to which they had long before agreed. The new program at Warkworth reduced the waiting list in eastern Canada from 150 to 135.

While the regional treatment centre at KP is treating about sixty sex offenders a year and Warkworth hopes eventually to match that number, the penitentiary treatment centres in Saskatchewan and British Columbia are ministering to an average of only forty-three and fifteen respectively. Together, all four programs can treat fewer than two hundred a year of the 1,400 sex offenders incarcerated in Canadian prisons.

Unlike their counterpart in Kingston, the treatment centres in Saskatoon and Abbotsford are accredited hospitals. They do not assess all sex offenders in their regions; their programs are completely voluntary. And although each program is based on roughly the same model, those in western Canada are longer: six months in Saskatoon, two years in Abbotsford.

Group therapy is a component of all four programs.

The clinicians have found that sex offenders are particularly effective at tearing away each other's rationalizations and forcing one another to face the facts. Sessions also focus on teaching the inmates basic sex education and social skills, such as how to be assertive, how to control anger, how to listen and converse. At Kingston Penitentiary, aversion treatment is used on an individual basis with inmates who have been identified as having deviant arousal patterns; when they feel themselves becoming excited by depictions of violent sex, for example, they are handed something putrid, like a rotting potato, to sniff or they are told to think about a negative image.

Since the early 1980s, the psychologists have been experimenting with various methods of getting offenders to empathize with their victims. It has been a bumpy road, according to Sharon Williams, the thirty-nine year old head of the sex offender unit at the Regional Treatment Centre at KP. Her first attempt, she says, was to invite a victim to address a group of inmates: "It was dreadful. They were angry that she would come in. They wanted to know what benefit it was to her—what she was getting out of watching them squirm. She dealt very well with it. But I thought, I will never put anyone through that again." The next time, Williams showed the offenders a tape of a victim, who was crying as she related her experience. The reaction was the same.

Gradually, it became clear that the timing of such sessions is as important as the information presented. Now the inmates are shown a variety of films that explore, in less intense fashion, victims' reactions to sexual assault, but not before they spend time exploring the factors that led to their own crimes. "It is not until they start to understand some of the things that led to their offending that they can be led into how other people feel," she says.

About forty percent of the sex offenders treated at KP are seen purely on an individual basis. In general, says Williams, these are men who either are not bright enough to benefit from group discussions or have specific problems that require a tailor-made approach. "In one case, I am dealing with an inmate who was abused for ten years of his life by a variety of people in positions of authority. He grew up unable to assert himself. During individual therapy, we can spend an hour honing in on that particular area."

Williams began working at KP seventeen years ago as a graduate student on contract, when she assisted Marshall in establishing the program for sex offenders. As she reflects on its evolution, she concedes that she misses one bygone component: "There was no coercive element to taking treatment in those days. . . . If anything, taking it put people more at risk when they returned to their parent institutions. Several [patients] were burned out of their cells when it became known that they were sex offenders. We attempted to disguise [the program's] intent by calling it special treatment services . . . unfortunately, spending four months here was enough to identify them.

"So, the only reason people came at that point was because they wanted to help themselves. I look back on those days in the mid-1970s as being probably the easiest from a therapeutic standpoint."

Technically, inmates imprisoned in Ontario today still volunteer for assessment. However, there is strong pressure on identified sex offenders to be tested. Those who refuse have little chance of getting one of the preferred jobs within their institution (working in the kitchen, for example), a transfer to a lower security institution, temporary absence passes or parole. Malcolm recalls a fifty-seven-year-old incest offender who was serving a two-and-a-half-year sentence at Warkworth when his mother died. He had not been through the assessment process; his request for an escorted pass to attend her funeral was turned down.

Ironically, the only chance a sex offender in eastern Canada has of getting parole is to be excused from treatment. The situation, says Graham Stewart, an Ontario official of the John Howard Society, is straight out of *Alice in Wonderland*. "What kind of disjointed thinking says either you release people early or you treat them?"

The inmates who undergo assessment are well aware that a recommendation for treatment virtually wipes out their chances for parole. Occasionally, says Malcolm, an offender will become so depressed after meeting with him, that he has to be placed in a special observation cell when he returns to the range to ensure that he doesn't commit suicide: "I had a guy like that recently. All because I said to him, 'I think you are going to benefit from some treatment.'"

The man was a first-time offender who had raped a woman he met in a bar. The assault occurred while he was walking her home after she rejected his drunken declaration of love.

"He thinks he has an alcohol problem," Malcolm says. "Well, certainly he does. There is no doubt about that. But he also has other problems. When I told him he was going to have to wait in prison another eighteen months for treatment . . . he said he was going to call his common-law wife and kids and tell them to fuck off. 'Why don't you let her decide whether she is willing to wait for you?' I asked him. He couldn't see that it had anything to do with her. It wasn't her choice. I said, 'This is one of the attitudes that you have to work on—your attitude toward women.' It absolutely infuriated him. He went storming out of here and back to his cell and pulled out all his pictures of his wife and children and ripped them up. Then he said he was going to kill himself."

Andre Huyghebaert understands well the frustration of waiting for treatment. The thirty-nine year old former military man was eligible for day parole in November 1987 after serving one year of a six-year sentence for rape and armed robbery. Two months later he was assessed at KP. Treatment was recommended and his name was added to the waiting list. At that point, he was twenty-first in line; six months later, he was seventy-sixth. In October 1988, Huyghebaert wrote David Cole, his Toronto lawyer: "I feel they are playing games with me here. I am entitled to the same health care while incarcerated as I would be out on the street, am I not? If I was on the street, I would not have to wait four years to avail myself of psychiatric treatment."

Later the same month, Huyghebaert applied for a temporary absence pass in order to be assessed for treatment at the Royal Ottawa Hospital; his request was denied. "In arriving at this decision," his classification officer wrote, "I have considered ... [your] need for treatment." It was a classic catch-22: he couldn't get an outside pass without treatment, but he couldn't get treatment without an outside pass. In the spring of 1989, the scenario was repeated. This time, Huyghebaert contacted Toronto's Clarke Institute of Psychiatry about being treated there. A psychologist from the institute interviewed the offender in prison. "I feel he meets the criteria for the assessment phase of the program," the assessor subsequently wrote to Cole. "I also explained to Mr. Huyghebaert that a final decision regarding his admission to the program would have to await the parole board's ruling regarding his suitability for parole."

By then, Huyghebaert had joined a dozen other Ontario sex offenders in suing the government. Their lawsuit maintains: "The principles of fair and equal access to treatment are regularly set aside in the administration of the waiting list in the interests of treating those closest to their mandatory supervision dates ... ahead of others who have been waiting longer to re-

ceive treatment but who have more time remaining on
their sentences. . . . The effect of this wait is to deny
those inmates seeking treatment the entitlements and
privileges normally accorded to all inmates in federal
penitentiaries."

Huyghebaert had spent sixteen years in the armed
forces when he raped a coworker in May 1986. He
staked out her secluded cottage on a weeknight when
he knew that her husband, who was stationed in another city, would not be there. At 10:00 P.M., a little
while after she had turned out the lights and gone to
bed, he cut the telephone lines leading to her residence
and broke in. She awoke to find a tall, thin man
wearing a dark wool ski mask carrying a knife standing
over her. When she screamed, he jumped on her and
held the knife to her throat. He covered her eyes with
tape and sexually assaulted her for four hours before
leaving. He was arrested the next day at his home.

Six weeks later, while he was awaiting trial, Huyghebaert robbed a bank to get some money to leave the
country. After camping out in the bush for two days, he
turned himself in to police. He subsequently pleaded
guilty to both offences. Presentence reports revealed that
he was the fifth of ten children who grew up with a
violent father in a two-bedroom house in the Prairies. He
left home at the age of sixteen, after completing grade
ten, and enrolled in a one-year electronics course. In
1970, he joined the armed forces. Before he was married,
he told a psychologist, he had ten girlfriends. Each of
them dropped him. Afterwards, he would fantasize about
beating them up. He said he had raped three of these
women; the first two did not report the crimes, and a
complaint by the third was not pursued by police.

Huyghebaert's career record was unblemished. In
fact, in the two years prior to this arrest, he received
one glowing performance report after another. In 1984,
for example, a superior noted: "MCpl. Huyghebaert is

a thorough, trustworthy individual who can overcome obstacles, secure cooperation from others and get the job done, without appealing to the boss for help. This NCO is eminently qualified for promotion to Sergeant now."

In sentencing him to prison, Judge C. James Newton of the District Court of Ontario strongly advised that Huyghebaert receive psychiatric treatment before being released. Several months later, when the judge was contacted by the parole board, he reiterated his recommendation.

By the fall of 1989, after serving three years in prison, Huyghebaert was still waiting. He couldn't get released without being treated; he couldn't get outside treatment without being released. "I've been yelling and screaming continually since I was sentenced to get treatment," he says. "When they started doing interviews for the program here [at Warkworth], I had my LU [living unit officer] call over and find out if I was going to be on it. The only answer I got back was that I am somewhere near the top of the list for the second program. But the people who are running the program don't have the final say on who goes on it. The administration here does. I've been a bit of a thorn in their sides, so in all probability, if they can stop it without getting any flak, they will. I know it. I have resigned myself to being here until November 1990, my mandatory supervision date. Then I expect they will probably try to detain me as a dangerous offender."

Huyghebaert's introduction to life on the inside came a couple of days after his court appearance while he was being transported to the reception centre at Millhaven maximum-security penitentiary. Out of the blue, he recalls, an inmate in shackles sitting across from him threw up his wrists and cracked him across the top of the mouth with the handcuffs. "I almost went unconscious."

His motivation for treatment inside the penitentiary system was at its highest point then, he says. "If you take an offender, any type of offender, first time around and you throw him into the system, he is scared. I'm not a coward. I've been in shooting situations in the military and the whole nine yards. I get into here, and I'm just bouncy. I know what I've done. That's when your feelings of remorse are the most because you are feeling sorry for yourself. You are thinking of what you did and the harm that you caused. And you want treatment because you don't ever want to come back into this environment."

Now, he says, prison holds no fear for him. "It's like a big Boy Scout camp. I've got no bills. I've got no worries. Nothing physical goes on unless you invite it. I've got my meals. I've got my room. I've got my entertainment.

"Once you've been in a prison, it is no longer a deterrent. You know what's there. You just coast from day to day. You've got absolutely no responsibilities. It's an ideal environment for someone who doesn't give a damn."

David Cole says many of his clients feel the same way. "For them, going to prison is time out. They get a rest. It's nicer. It's easier."

Huyghebaert continues, "They say they want the treatment to be fresh when you are released onto the street. To the inmates, and I imagine to most people, it makes a hell of a lot more sense to treat a person at the beginning of his sentence. Then, when he is eligible for parole, instead of giving him that ten-day wonder assessment that they give at RTC, they should put him into a thirty-day program . . . because in thirty days, you can't hide from a trained observer. . . . If there hasn't been a [positive] change, the guy doesn't get out."

If early treatment cannot be provided within the penitentiary system, says Huyghebaert, then sex offenders should be allowed to obtain it outside. "They say that the parole board doesn't have a mandate to release anybody on a conditional parole for treatment purposes because then the province will have to pay for it and not the federal government. [The provinces argue that the responsibility for the treatment of penitentiary inmates rests with the federal government.] My answer to that is, what's the difference? In the end, it is the Canadian taxpayer who pays for it."

Even if he is accepted into a penitentiary treatment program before he is released, Huyghebaert says he is growing cynical about how much can be accomplished in four months for a sex offender who has been imprisoned for years, particularly if there is no follow-up in the community. "They have told me, We don't care what you are; we are going to let you sit there and stew in your own juices for four years; then we are going to give you a four-month miracle program. Just like the TV evangelists and the laying on of hands. I'll be miraculously cured."

He intends to make his own arrangements for treatment when he is released. "I know I have to have someone to talk to," he says. "I know what I am capable of. I know my background, and I know the signs that will lead up to this happening again. I have to have an out. I have to be able to pick up the phone and call somebody and say, 'Look I need to come down and hash this out with you.'

"I kept things bottled up for years—things that happened in my past—for years and years and years. An old girlfriend of mine wrote me a letter when I was at Millhaven in reception. And I just poured it all out to her. It was the first time I had ever talked to anybody about it. Since then, I know I can talk about it, because I have. And I know that it lets . . . out that feeling of being nobody, being nothing, of being a piece of garbage.

"They say most sex offenders have low self-esteem.

I am very good at hiding that. I hide it from everybody. Except that I can't hide it from myself. I have to be up front with someone. At that point, I wasn't being upfront with anybody.

"I don't care if the parole board keeps me until the end of my sentence. The first thing I am going to do when I hit the street is to arrange to see a psychologist and just talk to him. Because I trusted my own instincts and my own control and it was not sufficient."

Huyghebaert says he was on a six-month drug binge when he raped his colleague. "So I know I also have to stay away from drugs." Otherwise, "because of my background, because of what has happened to me, if a certain situation develops, I am going to take advantage of it. I know it."

Sharon Williams agrees that it makes sense to treat inmates when they are most motivated—"when they remember their crimes with perfect clarity, when they remember the court situation, when they remember their parents' faces." But the resources are not available to do so. A survey of federal inmates in Ontario conducted for CSC in the summer of 1989, for example, showed that fifty-three percent of sex offenders—a third of whom had been released from prison—had received no treatment whatsoever for their deviancy. In addition, CSC's consultants reported, less than half of all inmates with a drug or alcohol problem had received treatment of any kind.

Since 1938, the federal government has established a plethora of royal commissions, task forces, parliamentary committees, advisory committees, and internal working groups to study the issue of treatment in federal penitentiaries. The call for greater emphasis on rehabilitation has grown stronger with each report. The royal commission in 1938 stated: "Nothing should be omitted which might improve the character of the prisoner. . . . Proper treatment should follow in an effort to remove the causes of his criminal tendencies. Quite apart from the humanitarian consideration, the question of greater national economy is involved here, because . . . the cost of maintaining a prisoner in the penitentiary is high and, if he can be cured, he ceases to be a charge on the state, and becomes instead an asset."

In 1956, the advisory committees began focusing specifically on the needs of sex offenders. The Fauteaux Report called on the government to remove sex offenders from the general prison population and conduct intensive research on their needs. Two years later, a royal commission reiterated the need for research and special facilities for the treatment of sex offenders. It noted that sexual psychopaths "appear to be treated in the same manner as any other prisoner. Although the provisions of the criminal code governing this class of offenders contemplate that they will receive special psychiatric treatment, facilities for such treatment are not available."

Two decades later, a parliamentary subcommittee reported that less than ten percent of sex offenders in federal prisons were receiving specialized treatment. Again, the government was exhorted to provide separate institutions for the treatment of sex offenders. Eleven years after that, in 1988, another parliamentary committee urged CSC to "dramatically increase the resources allocated to sex offender programs."

The federal government's response has been to order more reports. Following CSC's own internal investigation of the murder of Tema Conter and in advance of the public inquest into her death, it appointed a four-member board of inquiry headed by Toronto lawyer Jane Pepino to study the incident. On its heels, a working group of representatives from CSC, the solicitor-general, the National Parole Board and the Ontario Ministry of Correctional Services was established to examine sex offender programs in Canada. The ink was no sooner dry on the working group's fifty-one-page treatise when a number of prominent Canadians were named to a steering committee for yet another task force on the treatment of sex offenders.

The federal-provincial working group had already, like its many predecessors, clearly spelled out the deficits in the system: "It is evident that current programs are not adequate to provide treatment to all sex offenders who require it. . . . Continuity of treatment from the institution to the community is critical and currently problematic. . . . Outcome research is missing." And, like its forerunners, it presented a long list of recommendations to correct the problems.

Perhaps most telling, though, was the working group's observation that "There is no CSC national strategy for the management and treatment of sex offenders, nor is there a single office in National Headquarters which is responsible for the direction, policy and programs for sex offenders." To remedy the situation, it suggested that a special advisor on sex offenders, who commands respect from the professionals in the field, be appointed to the deputy commissioner of penitentiaries.

Bill Miles, the senior psychologist at the Regional Treatment Centre at KP, welcomes the suggestion. "The whole situation with regard to professionalism within CSC is terrible. We have just had a whole series of guidelines that were developed by bureaucrats." One of the authors, for example, has a background in plant management. "It is a bit like a society of butchers and veterinarians telling a doctor how to do her job. Here, we have administrators telling us not only what we shall do, but the way that we shall do it, and when we shall do it. This is bizarre. I've been writing to them for a year and a half now about it. But they don't understand what professionalism is about. We have ninety psychologists across the country, and we don't have a chief psychologist in Ottawa. We don't have even one in the regions."

What does that say about CSC's commitment to rehabilitation? "You don't have to be a philosophy major to work it out. If you don't accord it the basis of any sort of professional organization, you are not behaving in a manner in which you are likely to achieve your stated goal."

Miles' willingness to criticize his employer is unusual. CSC does not suffer detractors easily. In 1986, when parole officers were publicly protesting against the federal government's plan to privatize halfway houses—the plan has since been virtually abandoned—they were threatened with disciplinary action and filmed leaving their workplaces so that their clothes could later be matched to videos of masked demonstrators in Toronto. In 1988, when a citizens' advisory committee to CSC was also critical of its move to privatization, the group was abruptly disbanded, although in the face of a public outcry, it was quickly reinstated.

Miles is well aware of CSC's authoritarian nature. "It is an organization that lives in a world of blacks and whites. It can't tolerate the ambiguity of the greys that we all know are there. Certain types of personalities can't live with uncertainties. They have to resolve everything, one way or another. Right or wrong. It doesn't matter. The prison service gets more of those people than its share."

As he walks with a visitor past the building that serves as the punitive-segregation area at KP, Miles chuckles as he recalls an incident there several years ago. "The commissioner was here for a visit, and a couple of inmates got out and were standing on the roof as he walked by with the warden. It was very embarrassing. Wanting a quick solution, the warden yelled at the guards to get the hoses. Then he shouted to the inmates, 'Are you going to come down?' They refused. 'All right,' the warden said, 'turn on the hoses.' The guards did. A trickle of water dripped out."

In spite of the potential repercussions, Miles is known to speak his mind, even if his views do not coincide with those of his colleagues. He thinks, for example, that a disproportionate amount of the budget for psychological services in federal prisons is spent on sex offenders. "We have finite resources. If I have a department of eight and I put five of those psychologists in the sex offender unit, then I haven't got the resources to put into the mentally ill, into the mentally retarded, into the plain people who just want some counselling and that is probably all they need. I also don't have the resources to do ongoing monitoring."

The lack of longterm outcome studies is another of Miles' bugbears. "Most treatment situations are not based on solid scientific facts. The empirical data are not there." As a learning theorist, he says, he believes that since a sex offender's behaviour is probably learned, it can be unlearned. "But, by God, you've got to demonstrate it.

"If you want the bottom line," says Miles, "there isn't much of a commitment to truth or to searching for truth." Careful science is anathema to politicians because it takes so long. "Politicians have to have something to say, and they have to say it now. . . . It is not very satisfying to [tell voters] that they have to wait ten years for the answers."

Miles believes that politics is also behind the disparity of CSC's psychological-treatment resources across Canada. "British Columbia has 1,400 inmates and 135 beds. The Prairie Provinces have about 2,200 inmates and 120 beds. In Ontario, we have 3,000 inmates and 80 beds. There are another 750 prisoners in the Atlantic Provinces; we have one bed here for them. If someone is going to get more resources than me, then I am happy for them. But there doesn't seem to be any rational basis for it."

It is currently a semantic argument, though. Since

the "Stanton incident," prison psychologists across Canada now spend most of their time doing risk assessments to help the parole board determine when sex offenders and other inmates should be released.

While it can be argued that incarcerated sex offenders pose the greatest risk to public safety, they represent a small percentage of the total number of rapists and child molesters in Canadian society. Most have never seen the inside of a federal penitentiary or provincial jail, and they bear little resemblance to such hardened criminals as Melvin Stanton or Clifford Olson. In fact, they appear quite ordinary.

4

Profile of a Sex Offender

IT IS NINE O'CLOCK on a typical Monday morning at the Kingston Sexual Behaviour Clinic. Inside the old red-brick row house, which is sandwiched between students' quarters on the periphery of Queen's University's main campus, a psychologist awaits his first patient of the day. More than a thousand sex offenders from across Ontario have attended the clinic over the past fifteen years. Roughly a quarter of them, like the man the therapist is expecting, have been referred by a probation officer. The others have been sent by children's aid societies, lawyers and doctors, hospitals and mental health centres, family court judges, and the police. On rare occasions, a rapist or child molester has sought help at the clinic on his own.

The man expected this morning has pleaded guilty in provincial court to sexually molesting his neighbour's

ten year old daughter. An assessment of the offender's
sexual proclivities is required for a presentence report.

The therapist checks the clock; it is five past nine.
While he waits, he rereads the briefing notes sent to
him by the probation officer and frowns. The memo
states that the offender is thirty-eight years old, married and has children. He is a conscientious worker who
owns his own decorating business, and he has no record
of any previous sexual offences. The memo does not
have enough detail. Without the usual police report,
including a statement by the victim, the psychologist
has little information to challenge the man if he attempts, as most sex offenders do, to downplay or deny
his crime. Instead, he will have to look for inconsisten-
cies in his story.

At fifteen minutes after the hour, a tall, fair-haired
man lumbers through the doorway of the modest second-
floor office. His head is lowered. "I'm Graham," he
announces, offering no explanation for his lateness. His
jeans and heavy boots are splattered with paint, and his
T-shirt reads "Hunters make good lovers." Introduc-
tions over, Graham slouches into a chair across from his
assessor and remarks, with unmistakeable resentment,
that he has had to take off work for an entire morning to
attend the clinic, leaving an employee in charge of two
separate jobs. He wouldn't be here if his probation
officer had not ordered him to be, he says, and his
business might suffer from his absence. Not only is this
appointment costly to him, he adds, it won't be of any
use to the court because he doesn't have a problem.

The psychologist points out that Graham has been
convicted of sexually assaulting a child. The patient
agrees but says he simply fondled the girl and only on
one occasion. But the notes state that he pleaded guilty
to having oral sex with the ten year old five times
during a three-month period. "Yes," says Graham, "but
that is because my lawyer advised me that the court

would be easier on me if I did not contest the details."
So far, the assessment has proceeded in a predictable
manner. Few clients admit to all the allegations against
them initially, and seventy to eighty percent maintain
complete innocence.

As the interview continues, Graham begins to relax
and his surliness fades. With gentle coaxing, he starts to
reveal details of his life. He has a few male friends but
no one to whom he feels particularly close. His marriage is distant and he shares little in the way of leisure
activities with his wife. Long hours at work keep him
away from home, he says, although in a subsequent
interview, he admits that he often stays late at his job to
avoid spending time with his family. He resents the
obligations of marriage and says he wants to enjoy
himself after a long day and not have to cater to the
needs of his wife or children. He expresses no sympa-
thy for the burden his wife has to carry in looking after
the house and the family alone. That is her job, he
declares. He says he has sex with his wife about three
times a week but it is boring.

Graham's answers to a series of questionnaires
reveal that he is prudish in his attitudes toward sex but
desires a number of activities he considers to be deviant, such as oral-genital sex. He also desires sex with
children, whom he believes can be sexually provocative
and whom he doubts are harmed by having sex with an
adult. Although his responses indicate he can be assertive and even aggressive on some occasions, he is also
anxious and lacking in confidence.

Twice during the following week, Graham under-
went phallometric testing. The methods used at the
clinic are similar to those employed in Kingston Penitentiary, but the surroundings are far less spacious. The
offender sits on a brown plaid reclining chair behind a
curtained partition and places a strain gauge over his
penis. Directly in front of him is a television monitor;

above that is a slide projector and a video camera. In an adjacent room, one of the staff psychologists switches on the computer and starts the slide projector.

The tests are individualized. In Graham's case, he watched a series of males and females from three age categories: prepubescent, pubescent and adult. Each was naked and standing or sitting alone. In random order, the pictures were projected onto the screen for two minutes apiece; after every image, the screen went blank for two minutes. Following the slides, Graham watched four soundless, two-minute videotapes. Two depicted consenting sex between a man and a woman; two were scenes of a man engaged in sexual activity with a young girl. While the images appeared on the television set, a video camera trained on Graham's face ensured he was, in fact, watching the tapes and not averting his eyes to avoid becoming aroused.

The physiological assessments demonstrated that Graham was highly aroused by adult females, moderately aroused by prepubescent girls, and not at all aroused by males. Presented with the results, the offender expressed surprise that his sexual excitement to female children was measurable but, in the face of the evidence, acknowledged for the first time that he did have a problem. And he admitted that the five assaults he disclosed to the court were actually an underestimate of his sexual contacts with the girl. He still wanted to make excuses, however. He claimed that he had never thought about having sex with children until one evening when his wife asked him to look after their children and their neighbour's daughter. He could not explain exactly why he molested the child, but he volunteered that he was angry at having to baby-sit during his few free hours and he wanted to strike out at someone. It gave him a feeling of satisfaction, he recalled, even though he did not have an orgasm. Subsequently, he mastur-bated while thinking about the episode, and eventually, he began actively to seek out opportunities to be with the little girl.

Graham's case portrays a rather ordinary man who is successful in business but unhappy at home. Like many other sex offenders, he appears superficially to be a good provider, husband, and father. In reality, he is self-centred, resents the responsibilities of marriage, and has little or no intimacy in his life. The assumption, however, that all sex offenders fit his general description or, for that matter, any generic profile, is fallacious.

Among the offenders who have attended the Kingston Sexual Behaviour Clinic, the youngest is eleven; the oldest, seventy-eight. In general, it is rare to find a rapist outside the fifteen-to-forty-year age bracket; however, child molesters span a much broader age range. The details of four more case files will help to demonstrate the vast differences in the backgrounds, attitudes, and behaviour of sex offenders.

Gary was referred to the clinic from a psychiatric hospital where he admitted himself after he began to fantasize about cutting up little girls. An average-looking man of twenty-five years, he had medium-brown hair and longish sideburns. He appeared clean but somewhat unkempt. He did not shave daily, and his heavy cotton pants and long-sleeved shirts, which he kept buttoned up to the neck, were never pressed.

Unlike Graham, Gary readily admitted his problem. In fact, as he paced nervously around the psychologist's office during his first visit, he impressed the therapist with his obvious sincerity and distress. He had grown up in a poor family, he said, and dropped out of school after grade six. He worked in the evenings as a janitor and lived alone. He had never had a sexual relationship with a woman, but since puberty, he had been sexually molesting both girls and boys ranging in age from four to eight. Over the years, he had become so preoccupied with thoughts of sex that he found it difficult to concentrate on anything else.

His whole life was built around pursuing opportunities to be alone with children, he said. Every day before he went to work, he hustled youngsters in playgrounds, in pinball arcades, anywhere they were to be found. He had lost track of exactly how many he had molested, but estimated the number to be well in excess of two hundred. When there were no children around, he cut out pictures of young girls and boys from newspapers and popular magazines and pored over his small collection of child pornography. His fantasies of women and girls included vaginal intercourse, and his favourite daydream involved setting up house with an eight year old girl. His images of boys were limited to oral sex. If he could not rid himself of all these thoughts, he said, he would commit suicide.

Despite his bizarre reveries, he did not appear to the psychologist to be mentally unstable. He gabbled but was coherent and seemed brighter than his education would suggest.

Gary's responses to the clinic's questionnaires revealed a man afraid of interacting with anyone, but particularly anxious about whether he would be a satisfactory lover if given the opportunity with a woman. He was unassertive and had never experienced emotional intimacy with anyone. In the laboratory tests, Gary was aroused by all the stimuli presented to him, indicating he was bisexual. The results also showed that the thought of physically injuring his sexual partners did not inhibit him.

For the next fourteen months, Gary remained in the hospital and visited the clinic twice a week for group and individual therapy. Although his problems were more serious than many of the clinic's patients, his determination to overcome them, combined with the intensity of his treatment, eventually prevailed.

Follow-up has revealed that the man has lived in his home community for nearly ten years without any sign of reoffending.

The next two case histories are of men who assaulted teenage and adult women. Again, their problems and crimes are markedly different.

Brian was twenty-one years old when he was referred to the clinic by his lawyer. He and a male friend were charged with raping a fourteen year old girl. Brian's lawyer believed he was innocent and thought that phallometric testing would show he had no abnormal sexual proclivities, which would help his case. The victim told police that the three had met at a party and had gone to an apartment together to listen to records. Once there, she said, both men forced her to have vaginal intercourse with them and then to fellate them. While holding her captive for more than two hours, they also forced a beer bottle into her vagina and Brian's companion had anal intercourse with the terrified girl.

Brian held a responsible job at a bank where he had worked for three years since graduating from high school. On his first visit to the clinic, he wore a suit. Noticing the staff's casual attire, he dressed down for subsequent appointments, but he was always impeccably clothed. He came from a middle-class background, was good-looking, intelligent, articulate, and at times even arrogant.

Testing showed Brian to be assertive, self-confident, and free of anxiety. There was slight evidence that he was aroused by forced sex, but no sign that he was excited by the thought of having sex with children. His strongest responses, in fact, were to scenes of consenting sex with an adult female. He denied during several interviews that he had raped the teenager. He was drunk that night, he said, but he clearly remembered he did not have intercourse with her. He did not have to. He had a girlfriend and had had sex with her the very afternoon of the day the alleged offence occurred.

Brian described sexual relations with his girlfriend as pleasurable and claimed he enjoyed the times he spent with her. But he said he had his best times drinking with his buddies. His responses to the questionnaires indicated that he held extremely negative views of women; he thought some deserve to be raped, and he considered the trauma of the offence to be greatly exaggerated. Although he trivialized rape in abstract terms, he steadfastly maintained his own innocence.

When forensic evidence presented at his trial proved his semen was in the teenager's vagina, in a sudden turnaround, he not only admitted his part in the current crime, he confessed to police that he had sexually assaulted three other young women in the previous two years. With one conviction against him, he reasoned that his past would catch up with him. He had a better chance of being dealt with leniently, he thought, if he declared his guilt and accepted his punishment for all four crimes at once. He was sentenced to eighteen months in jail. He said he did not want any treatment.

Kenneth presented quite a different picture. He was a soft-spoken man in his late forties who owned a hardware store. He was referred to the clinic by his family physician after a twenty-three-year-old female clerk who worked for him complained to police that he had touched her breasts and buttocks on three separate occasions in one week. The woman had worked at the store for two years and said until that time, her employer had been pleasant and respectful. Kenneth agreed with her account of the incidents and expressed considerable remorse for his actions.

An analysis of Kenneth's sexual responses showed only minimal arousal to any stimuli, and he candidly told the interviewer that he had experienced very little sexual interest since his wife left him five years earlier. He was a quiet, private person who said he kept busy with his work and, until recently, felt fulfilled. Two months before the offences, however, his sales dropped so low that he was in danger of having to close his business. In an attempt to save it, he borrowed money to renovate the store's exterior and to buy television advertising. He said he was under extreme stress when he molested his employee.

A man like Kenneth may commit only one sexual offence in his lifetime. At the other extreme are sex offenders who become addicted to fulfilling their deviant fantasies, and their crimes frequently show a progressively violent trend. Warren is one of these men. When he was first assessed at the Kingston clinic in 1972 at the age of twenty-eight, he had been arrested for exposing his genitals and peeping in women's windows. He was married and reported enjoying sexual and social relations with his wife, although she did not share his perspective. Testing uncovered no deviant tendencies. In fact, Warren appeared to be much like most other men except that he was markedly underassertive and attempted to buy friendships through favours and gifts. He was a tradesman and would spend days, for example, rewiring an acquaintance's house for free. When his attempts to ingratiate himself with people did not work, he became resentful and angry. Treatment was aimed at getting him to become more assertive and self-confident. He was not interested in changing his behaviour, however. He had been sent to the clinic as a term of his probation and, as soon as he could, he quit.

Five years later, Warren molested an eight year old girl while on probation for breaking and entering and was referred again for assessment at the clinic by his probation officer. He was more assertive this time, even occasionally obnoxious. But now, he was beginning to look scruffy and was more socially anxious: he sat on the edge of his seat during his assessment and fidgeted. His wife had left him two years before, and he had lost his job at the same time. He was a homely man, yet he boasted that many women were interested in his body. Intellectually, he was at the low end of the normal range, but he often talked of the grandiose plans he had for his life. Phallometric tests indicated that Warren was no longer repulsed by deviant sexual behaviour. He was aroused by scenes of sex with female children and, to a lesser extent, of forced sex. He spent two months in individual treatment this time—his therapist tried to get him to recognize that he had a serious problem that was getting progressively worse—but, again, he participated only half-heartedly. He left after two months, saying he was cured; his opinion was not shared by his therapist.

The third time Warren was assessed by a psychologist from the clinic, he was in jail. He had been arrested for viciously raping a female patient at a psychiatric hospital where he worked as a volunteer. On the pretext of taking the woman for an afternoon drive in the country, he drove to a secluded spot, forced her at knife-point to undress, raped her, and then made her fellate him. Before abandoning her, he pushed a screwdriver into her vagina and anus and urinated on her.

In the three-year interval since he was last seen by staff from the clinic, he had worked for only brief intervals and had spent a short time in jail on two break-and-enter convictions. He felt lonely and alienated and mistreated by everyone. He couldn't understand why he couldn't keep a job, friend or even an apartment once his record became known. Since he had spent time in jail, he thought, his offences should be forgotten. By now he had lost all regard for his appearance and was dirty and unshaven. Testing showed he was highly aroused by all deviant themes: sex with children, rape, peeping and exposing, and various sadistic acts. He believed that women want to be raped and that children enjoy sex with adults.

Warren's profile at each of his assessments shows essentially three different men. Such dramatic changes are not typical of untreated—or unsuccessfully treated—sex offenders, but it is common to see an acceleration, over time, in their arousal to deviant acts. A child molester, for example, may begin by simply fondling his victims; some years or children later, he might attempt intercourse. Similarly, a rapist may use only enough force to achieve his sexual goal the first time, but savagely beat his third or fourth victim. As the seriousness of the crimes accelerates, there is a corresponding change in the offenders' attitudes as they attempt to rationalize their behaviour.

Research has shown that as many as two-thirds of all men admit at least some likelihood that they would force a woman into unwanted sexual acts if they were sure they could get away with it. This statistic underlines the difficulty clinicians face in providing a profile of a sex offender. Clearly, the stereotypical image of a demented, physically repulsive man lurking in the bushes in a rumpled raincoat is far from reality. Many rapists and child molesters are respected members of society. Most are reasonably attractive. Some are downright handsome. And very few—less than two percent of convicted rapists, for example—are psychotic, or crazy.

Clinicians who treat sex offenders are frequently asked what type of person commits these crimes. The easiest answer is men. Less than three percent of all individuals charged with sex offences are women, and even then, many of these female offenders are the accomplices of males rather than the actual perpetrators. There are, to be sure, some women who seek out children for sexual pleasure, but they are rare.

Although sex offenders who are imprisoned tend to

be unemployed, unskilled or semiskilled workers who have poor educations and few social graces, this is most likely due to the selective nature of the investigative and judicial process. Offenders from disadvantaged social classes are simply more likely to be charged, convicted and incarcerated than men from more privileged ranks in society. There are many examples of this bias and the attitudes that foster it in Chapter 7.

The fact that offenders from the middle and upper classes tend to get away with their crimes, at least initially, has the effect of perpetrating the myth that sex offenders are vastly different from all other males. They are not. Indeed, there is little that sets sex offenders apart from other men. They come from every educational, economic, and social stratum. In 1989 alone, for example, thirty priests and other officials of the Roman Catholic Church were charged with sex offences involving children; nine were Christian Brothers affiliated with the Mount Chasel orphanage in Newfoundland. In Quebec, the former coach of a junior hockey team was charged with seven counts of sexually assaulting boys. In Ontario, a forty-five year old high school teacher was arrested in connection with forty-four sex crimes against teenage girls. In Manitoba, a former provincial magistrate was sent to jail for sexually assaulting his two young children over a four-year period. In Alberta, a small-town mayor, who was also a probation officer, was convicted of sexually assaulting an eighteen year old male parolee; a YMCA camp counsellor, a doctor, and two police officers in Alberta were also arrested on charges of sexual assault. In British Columbia, a fundamentalist preacher was incarcerated for sexually assaulting female parishioners during a ritual to purge them of demons.

Sex offenders may commit monstrous acts, but they do not appear to be monsters. Clifford Olson and Ted Bundy, the most notorious sex offenders in Canada and the United States respectively, perhaps best illustrate this point. Although Canadian newspapers seem to delight in running photographs of Olson looking unshaven and dishevelled, on most days, he bears no resemblance to the man in those pictures. Even though he spends twenty-three hours a day inside a protective custody cell at Kingston Penitentiary, he is usually clean-shaven and neatly dressed. He is at least moderately handsome, intelligent, and able to carry on an interesting and enjoyable conversation. Individuals who meet Olson without realizing who he is are typically shocked at how pleasant he can appear. Similarly, Bundy, the good-looking and articulate former law student, was widely admired by men and women alike. He was a Republican worker, a rape crisis volunteer, and one of America's most successful killers. It is one of the great ironies of sex offending that such men can use their charm to disarm not only their victims but often even the investigators of their gruesome crimes.

Sex offenders, like criminals in general, tend to be adept at manipulating others for their own ends, and they appear not to have internalized society's rules and morals. They are aware of the rules, but they have no respect for them. The very fact that sex offenders usually exercise great caution to avoid getting caught demonstrates that they know what they are doing. They are also prone to be self-centred and insensitive to their victims. Of course, to rape a woman or molest a child, a man must be able to ignore the distress of his victim. In sexual relations between two consenting adults, most males would lose their arousal if their partners expressed pain. And normal adults are upset when a child is suffering. Not so sex offenders. At least while they are committing the assault, they do not care about their victims' feelings. In some cases, their lack of empathy is shocking, even to clinicians used to working with them.

In March of 1982, six months after Duane Taylor

was arrested for sexually attacking and murdering two year old April Morrison, Bill Marshall was asked by Taylor's lawyer to do a second assessment of the man's sexual deviances. Marshall and an assistant interviewed the offender in the Brockville jail, where he was being held pending trial. To this day, Marshall recalls with sickening clarity the way that Taylor delighted in telling the professionals every last detail of his gruesome crime. The fact that Taylor himself looked like an innocent child made his story all the more horrific. As Marshall and his colleague drove the fifty miles back to Kingston on that cold spring afternoon, neither said a word. Both knew that if they tried to talk, they would not be able to hold back their tears.

Even though Taylor was borderline retarded, he was aware that what he had done was terribly wrong. He knew that people reviled him. And he recognized that he would be in danger of being killed by other inmates when he returned to the penitentiary. He did not care. Although his case is an extreme example of the lack of empathy exhibited by sex offenders, it is not uncommon for these men to say that their victims enjoyed being assaulted despite clear evidence to the contrary. One rapist at the Kingston clinic adamantly made this claim even though he admitted that his victim was crying and pleading with him to stop throughout the attack. The denial of the pain they have caused is part of the offenders' attempts to rationalize their behaviour.

Just as many rapists think that women secretly want to be raped and are deliberately provocative, child molesters will often say that their victims' actions made it clear they wanted sex. One pedophile told Marshall that he sexually assaulted his neighbour's young daughter while they were watching television because she pulled her feet underneath her, as children often do, and sat crosslegged in front of him, exposing her underpants. He saw this as a deliberate sexual invitation.

Similarly, if a victim of incest responds to her abuse by becoming promiscuous in her teens, her father often points to her behaviour as a clear confirmation that she played a provocative role in their sexual relations. Other fathers go so far as to maintain they were just showing their daughters love and teaching them about sex in a nice way.

While sex offenders tend to hold distorted views of their crimes and their victims and to lack empathy, there is no easy way to distinguish them from other men. They come in all shapes and sizes, from wealthy families and poor families, hold jobs ranging from unskilled labourers to professionals, and have personalities ranging from charismatic to withdrawn. This point cannot be stressed enough. As Ted Bundy said during a 1986 interview with *The New York Times*, "What people have to realize is that . . . in all significant respects, I am essentially like everyone else." Bundy's lawyer, James Coleman, commented, "He's your next-door neighbour. People don't want to believe that their next-door neighbour can behave like this. The reaction is, 'He's one of us, my God.'"

Women and children must recognize that sex offenders can appear respectable and may be well known to them. Professionals in the criminal justice system and in mental health services must accept that men belonging to their social class can and do rape women and molest children. Furthermore, these criminals can cause as much suffering as offenders who are unattractive, unskilled, uneducated or dull-witted. In fact, when apparently respectable sex offenders go free, the damage to their victims may be greater because no one believed the accusations. All too often, professionals, even in child protection agencies, make the mistake of assuming that a "respectable" offender either did not commit the offence or will never do it again; they also believe that these men do less harm to their victims. The following case illustrates this point.

Gordon was sent to the Kingston clinic towards the end of a two-year period of probation, for performing fellatio on a four-year-old boy. He had a stable marriage with two children, attended church regularly and was respected by his colleagues in the armed services, in which he had worked for ten years. After his arrest, Gordon sought out a psychiatrist and was in treatment until the time he was referred to the clinic by his probation officer. A report from the psychiatrist described the patient in glowing terms and said his problem was "that he did not wear the pants in the family." Accordingly, his treatment over the two years had been directed at making Gordon more dominant over his wife. When the clinic conducted its assessment, it was evident that Gordon was highly aroused by young boys and still at high risk to offend.

It is not only professionals who err in their judgements of seemingly respectable sex offenders. Their friends and families characteristically often refuse to believe the allegations, at least initially. When altar boys in St. John's, Newfoundland, first reported more than a decade ago that Reverend James Hickey had forced them to commit sexual acts with him, the boys and their families were rejected by the community for slandering the good priest. No one believed the complaints because Father Hickey was a priest in a small parish, with all the power and dignity that this job entailed. The fact that he was a member of the clergy not only protected him and other priests who have since been convicted of sexual assault, it may have bolstered a confidence in the offenders which led them to victimize even greater numbers of boys with a wider range of sexual behaviours.

Of course, if a sex offender's friends and family

consider him to be innocent or, at worst, to have made an uncharacteristic mistake, it is not surprising that professionals who see him for a brief period of time in unusual circumstances can make errors in judgement. However, individuals who are in a position to make judgements should be aware that whether a man seems to be of good character, holds a professional position, comes from a good family, or is popular is no indication of either his guilt or his subsequent risk to the community. Outward appearances mean nothing. There are no stereotypes. The fact that we like to believe there are is one reason so many sex offenders go free.

5

The Motives of
Sex Offenders

IN THE SUMMER of 1989, at the age of forty, Robert
Noyes sat across from a psychologist in a stark interview
room at Warkworth penitentiary and looked back on his
life. Three years earlier, the tall, handsome teacher had
been sentenced, in front of a packed British Columbia
courtroom, to an indeterminate prison term for sexually
assaulting nineteen children in five cities over fifteen
years. During the course of three long interviews,
Noyes recounted the events that eventually led to his
incarceration. He had a warm, open manner, and his
listener was increasingly impressed with his intelligence, his insight, and his genuine interest in ridding
himself of the deviant desires that had ruined his life.

Noyes grew up in a small city. A gangly only child,
he wore glasses and braces and felt unattractive and
uncoordinated. He didn't know how to interact with

other children and had no close friends. He had a good relationship with his mother but always felt that his father did not love him.

Noyes remembers his father as distant and unaffectionate—a successful journalist who loved mathematics and was a first-rate chess player. While young Robert craved the hugs and expressions of love he saw other fathers give their sons, the only interaction he had with his father was over the chess board. And that did not last long. The elder Noyes never allowed his son to win, and typically, the two were in fierce competition with one another. At the age of six, Robert threw the board over in frustration one day and stormed out of the room. It was the last time they played together. Sometime later, his father, plagued by anxiety and stress, turned to alcohol for consolation and became even more remote.

Leaning forward in his chair, tears welling in his eyes, Noyes related how, when he was an adult, his father called him to his side when he was dying in the hospital and said he was sorry he had never shown his son any love when he was a child. He really had loved him, his father insisted.

When he was thirteen years old, Noyes was playing alone in his driveway one winter afternoon when his nine-year-old neighbour, Wayne, came by. Convinced Wayne was staring at him because he was weird, Robert threw a snowball at him. But Wayne spoke to Robert anyway and seemed eager to join him. Robert was amazed. "Hey," he thought, "this kid likes me." The two played together for a while and finally took to wrestling in the snow. Robert found the close contact enjoyable, much as he imagined it would be if his father hugged him. As they rolled about, he felt an unfamiliar but pleasant sensation in his groin. Within moments, he ejaculated for the first time. Thinking he had wet his pants, he ran into the house, embarrassed. When he removed his clothing, he realized what had happened.

Over the next few days, Robert vividly recalled the pleasure he had felt embracing Wayne and tried to recreate the feelings in the privacy of his own room by masturbating. At every opportunity during the next month or so, he would initiate a wrestling match with Wayne. One day, the two were playing in the basement when Robert got an idea for the perfect game. He told Wayne he had a penny in his pocket. If Wayne could find it, he could have it. As Wayne's groping fingers touched Robert's erect penis, Robert ejaculated. Thereafter, Robert's behaviour became more explicit. One day Wayne's mother, who obviously had somehow been made aware of what was happening, forbade Robert to play with her son. No one made any attempt to correct his behaviour, however.

Two years later, at the age of fifteen, Noyes found himself alone with the younger brother of a friend. He repeated the penny game. From then on, he sought out opportunities to be alone with young boys.

When he was nineteen years old, Noyes says, he had his first sexual experience with a woman. It was a disaster. He was insecure, and she was ambivalent. By the time she resolved to go ahead, he was impotent. Devastated, he left her and walked aimlessly through a deserted park, weeping. He saw himself as a sexual failure and blamed his earlier involvement with boys. He had never heard the term homosexual pedophile, but he felt that something was terribly wrong and he wanted to die. The cycle had begun, however. Robert turned to young boys for affection and consolation, as he would continue to do for the next fifteen years, whenever he was under stress. He still dated women, but he backed out of relationships with them when sex became inevitable.

When he was thirty-one years old, Noyes married

and had two children. But still, he reacted to the problems and anxieties in his life by fondling boys, who by then were students at the schools in which he taught. In choosing his targets, he sought out youngsters who were everything he had wanted to be as a child—good-looking, popular, sports stars. As time went on and the age discrepancy between Noyes and his victims became more like that of father and son, he tried to give the boys what he had missed. He showered them with the attention and affection that his father never gave him. And, with those who would cooperate, he had sex, typically mutual masturbation. With deep remorse, he later recalled how he had talked himself into believing that he was not harming these boys; he was only giving them the type of pleasure he had experienced with Wayne many years earlier.

While a sex offender's own account of his motives is useful in attempting to understand not only the individual's behaviour but deviant sexual practices generally, it does not provide the whole story. Even in the course of therapy, an offender is acutely aware that he is relating his actions and feelings to someone who will make judgements about him. He may be trying to be as honest as possible, but his account is only as good as his memory. And all of us remember events in a manner that both makes sense of the past and puts us in the most favourable light.

Any attempt at identifying the motives of sex offenders, therefore, remains somewhat speculative. However, there are certain recurring patterns and internal characteristics that prompt these men to offend in the first place and to continue to do so even though they fully realize that their actions are wrong and that they will probably be caught eventually.

Although humans are born with a propensity to engage in sexual behaviour, no one is born a rapist or a pedophile. Our sexual preferences are learned through our social conditioning and our individual experiences. How much impact each experience has depends both on when it occurs and on our vulnerability at the time. At puberty, for example, the hormones that drive male sexual urges increase five-fold within two years. During this period, boys go from being almost asexual to being virtually preoccupied with sexuality. This is a time when they will be particularly susceptible to sexual messages and experiences.

If a boy has been abused or neglected during his childhood, he will either seek out experiences that enhance his feeling of self-worth or respond strongly to such experiences when they fortuitously occur. Almost any event that makes him feel both sexually aroused and powerful will have a strong impact. Since boys from emotionally deprived backgrounds also tend to be socially anxious and awkward, especially with girls, they will often be particularly attracted to sexual experiences that require little or no social effort on their part.

The portrait of Robert Noyes suggests that at least three motives were involved in his early sexual abuse of boys: sexual desire, a yearning for physical contact, and a need for love. The accidental association of sexual arousal and physical contact with Wayne was so enjoyable to the inexperienced boy that it produced a desire to repeat the behaviour. This desire was increased by masturbation and then entrenched with repeated partners. If Noyes' first sexual encounter had been with a girl of his own age, his life might have been entirely different.

The process of establishing sexual preferences is the same for deviant and normal sex. When thoughts of a particular behaviour are paired with sexual pleasure, the desire for the behaviour increases. In time, the person may either seek out opportunities to engage in his preferred sexual practice or, at least, take advantage of the opportunity when it arises. In a few offenders, their sexual desires become so obsessive that they occupy much of their daily planning.

A sexual desire for young boys was clearly one of the motives that Noyes had for molesting children. But why did he respond to that single incident with Wayne by developing deviant desires? Many pubescent males become aroused wrestling with other boys and do not develop an attraction to them. Obviously, Noyes had other needs that were satisfied by his contact with Wayne, which made the experience uniquely powerful.

All of us are exposed to an enormous amount of information at every moment of our lives, but we respond to only a small segment of it. What we react to depends on how we are feeling at the time. If we are hungry and stop at the supermarket on our way home from work, we notice everything on the food stands and consider most of it essential for our evening meal. If we are not hungry, we do not even see the custard pie, for example, or, if we do, it does not seem so strongly tempting.

When Noyes had the unexpected experience with Wayne, he was lonely and lacking in physical affection. His close contact with Wayne served to heighten the importance of the accompanying sexual arousal. The fact that Wayne wanted to play with him underlined the salience of the contact.

Later, other motives were added. After he failed in his first sexual experience with a female, Noyes began to fear relationships with women, making sex with alternative partners attractive. A crucial part of his self-definition came to be his secret attraction to boys; this made him different from other people and increased his sense of alienation.

Many sex offenders, though certainly not all, had dreadful childhoods. Some were beaten, others were sexually abused and still others, like Noyes, were rejected by crucial people in their lives. These experiences make individuals feel unworthy, unlovable, cheated and resentful, if not downright hostile. Other offenders had apparently good childhoods but suffered some serious setback later in their lives. When under severe stress, they were vulnerable to what might otherwise have been an ignored opportunity to have sex with a child or to force a woman to submit to their sexual advances.

Not all individuals respond either to poor childhoods or to severe stresses by becoming sex offenders. Some, in the pursuit of self-esteem, become workaholics. Others sink into the oblivion of alcohol, and so on. To some extent, circumstances determine which path we follow. But whatever our choice, if the experience is rewarding, we tend to re-create it. With sex offenders, sooner or later, their deviant sexual practices increasingly become the way in which they respond to any feelings of deprivation or distress, until the smallest upset signals the need to engage in aberrant sex and the slightest effort indicates deprivation and the need for a reward.

Albert's case illustrates how a combination of factors can suddenly lead a man to commit a sex offence. The twenty-nine year old tradesman was referred to the Kingston Sexual Behaviour Clinic after he was charged with sexually assaulting two young girls. He had had a normal childhood and a history of satisfactory sexual relations with various women, although every relationship had ended with Albert being rejected. Albert told a psychologist that he had never even thought of molesting a child until the first time that he did. Indeed, prior to his own offence, he said, he was repulsed by the idea and believed that child molesters were "creeps" whom he would be able to recognize.

The first offence occurred after a long afternoon and evening of drinking and watching strippers in several hotels with two buddies. At closing time, the trio went to visit friends. Albert agreed, when asked, to baby-sit their eleven-year-old daughter, who was still awake, while everyone else went out. He was intoxicated, lonely, and depressed. His last girlfriend had left him some months earlier, and he was afraid of being rejected by another woman. He settled in to watch an X-rated movie on television. As the young girl chatted to him in a friendly manner, he noticed that, when she moved, he could see her underpants under her short nightie. Within half an hour, he had made a pass at her and begun to fondle her genitals.

For the next three months, Albert was constantly afraid that people could tell just by looking at him that he was a child molester. He thought that his girlfriends had left him because they knew he was a potential offender, even though he himself had not been aware of it. Over time, however, Albert rationalized his behaviour and convinced himself that the young girl had enjoyed his advances. This removed his negative feelings, and he began to masturbate to his memories of the incident. Eventually, he molested another child. This time, the girl told her parents, who called the police.

Why some men rape women or molest children is as difficult to analyse as it is to describe the offenders themselves. The reasons are complex and, to some extent, different for each person. However, as discussed in the previous chapter, many sex offenders hold distorted views of their crimes and lack empathy with their victims. They also tend to share other internal characteristics that set them apart from other men. To explore these, we will consider the various categories of sex crimes, since it is reasonable to assume that their motives are not all the same. We would not expect a sadist, for example, who gains sexual pleasure from torturing, mutilating and murdering his victim, to have the same motives as a man who fondles the genitals of a single child.

Although sex may seem to be the most obvious

motive for sex crimes, most sex offenders are not overwhelmed by their sexual drive. Sex is, for example, only occasionally the primary motive in rape. Research has shown that although sadists, who constitute about ten percent of rapists, do tend to have abnormally high testosterone levels (the hormonal basis of sexual desire) and consequently desire sexual release more often, most rapists do not. Sadistic rapists differ from other rapists in more than one way, though. Ron Langevin, a research psychologist at the Clarke Institute of Psychiatry in Toronto, has demonstrated that sadistic rapists are hostile individuals who feel strong sexual arousal only when sexual acts include cruelty. For reasons that remain unclear, some of them also derive sexual pleasure out of dressing in women's clothing. These men are typically loners who have a history of childhood brutality to animals. Studies have also shown that sadists usually develop their deviant tendencies in early adolescence and participate in more bizarre behaviours than other sex offenders.

The need to reduce sexual urges is more frequently the primary motivation in the sexual assault of children, although fewer than ten percent of child molesters are sadists. But even here, the nature of the sexual motive is complex. The majority of men who sexually assault young girls, for example, are not true pedophiles, according to recent research pioneered by Kurt Freund of the Clarke Institute. In other words, they do not show the highest sexual arousal, in phallometric tests, to depictions of sex with children. This is particularly true of incest offenders, fifty-five percent of whom demonstrate the greatest attraction to sex with an adult female. According to the latest study of the Kingston Sexual Behaviour Clinic, of men who sexually abuse other people's daughters, forty-five percent would rather have a woman as a sexual partner; fifteen percent show equal arousal to sex with children and women, and forty percent show a preference for sex with children.

When the Kingston researchers studied men who molest boys, the results were even more surprising. Not only were most not pedophiles, according to physiological assessments, two-thirds were not homosexual. The heterosexuals who molested boys, all of whom were under age eleven, admitted they were attracted by their soft skin and their small penises. But they said they approached boys because they were less likely to arouse suspicion by spending time with them than with young girls.

Few sex offenders report feeling compelled to engage in high rates of sexual activity. In one study at the Kingston clinic, forty-one percent of nonoffending men said they masturbated more than twice a week, compared with forty percent of child molesters and fifty percent of rapists. Furthermore, almost twenty percent of the sex offenders said they desired sex less than once a week, whereas only eight percent of the nonoffenders were so disinterested in sexual release.

Sexual drive, evidently, is not the only reason that sex offenders commit their crimes. All men engage in sexual behaviour for a variety of reasons other than the pure pursuit of orgasm. Normal men have sex because it is pleasurable, to be sure, but they also do so out of habit and because it enhances their self-confidence. Engaging in sex also confirms the bond between a man and his sexual partner and may be one of the few ways in which some men can show their partners affection. And for many men, sex is the only expression of intimacy.

Nicholas Groth, an American psychologist who has achieved international renown for his research into, and treatment of, sex offenders, believes that rape and child molestation are pseudo-sexual crimes—that they are enacted for reasons other than sexual desire. By overpowering a woman or dominating a child, Groth says, rapists and pedophiles are trying to assert their masculinity. While other studies have shown that only a small percentage of offenders lack confidence in their maleness, Groth does seem to be correct in pointing to the obvious pleasure that both rapists and child molesters derive from the power imbalance inherent in their assaults.

For many men, sex is one of the main indicators of their masculinity, which no doubt explains why some tend to be so boastful about their sexual exploits. But sex can also make them feel powerful in other ways. It can offset feelings of inadequacy induced by other people in their lives by making them feel dominant over their partners. Some men refuse to have intercourse unless they are on top of the woman because in any other position, they lose their sense of power and feel vulnerable.

For rapists, this sense of power seems to be the most prominent motive for their crimes. Among incarcerated rapists, who have been well studied, the desire for power is often mixed with strong hostility towards women. Often, rapists can identify specific women to whom they feel particularly antagonistic.

Several years ago, Howard Barbaree, a psychologist and associate director of the Kingston Sexual Behaviour Clinic, assessed a rapist like this at Kingston Penitentiary. Fred expressed quite different emotions towards three women in his life. He said he hated his ex-wife, who left him when he was arrested. He mildly resented a woman friend, who kept in touch with his ex-wife. And he loved his current girlfriend, a woman he met while in prison. Fred's sexual responses were tested in relation to several scenarios involving a man and a woman. Barbaree described different situations depicting a woman enthusiastically participating in sex, being raped, or simply being beaten by the man. He varied the identity of the woman in each scene.

When the woman portrayed was his girlfriend, Fred showed the greatest arousal when she was enthusiastic and consenting, little response when she was raped, and none when she was beaten. When the woman was identified as his ex-wife, however, Fred's reaction was the opposite. He was fully aroused by the pure physical assault, partially by the rape scene, and not at all by the consenting scenario. His responses to scenarios involving the woman he mildly resented were halfway between the two extremes.

For rapists, exercising power over a woman serves to enhance their feelings of masculinity and self-esteem. But it also meets other needs. Even in Fred's rare case, where his hostility was completely fused with his sexual feelings, raping women also met his desire for revenge against his ex-wife, whom he perceived to have deserted him when he needed her most. For most rapists, the desire for vengeance is not so clearly focused. Sometimes a rapist hates women because he considers he has been injured by a particular woman or several women. Other times, rapists feel the whole world has treated them badly; they express their general need for revenge against society towards females because they are easier targets than men.

In the National Film Board documentary film *Why Men Rape*, one incarcerated rapist explains, "I still hate to say it. I hate to admit it. But I hated women. That is the feeling I felt, a rage." Another comments, "I think now that the real reason I committed my crime is that I felt very inferior to others. I felt rotten about myself. And by committing rape, I took this out on someone at that time that I thought was weaker than me—someone who I could control."

It is worth noting here that among the theories put forth over the years by psychoanalysts is the belief that men sexually attack women and children because of some problem they encountered with their own mothers when they were young. According to this view, because their mothers somehow hindered their growing independence and self-confidence, sex offenders either hate women or fear them. Hatred turns them into rapists; fear turns them into child molesters.

This Freudian-based analysis, which holds women responsible for sex crimes and turns offenders into victims, is not only offensive but misguided. There are many paths to fear and hatred. A more plausible explanation for the hostility expressed by some rapists and the timidity of some child molesters is their general lack of social skills, especially in conversations with females. In general, individuals who are poor conversationalists tend to be anxious about interacting with others, and some respond with hostility to hide their problems. In addition, the characteristic way in which women are portrayed in the popular media, in advertising, and in pornography, tends to encourage men to feel hostile towards women. Indeed, research has shown that men who say they would force a woman into unwanted sexual acts if they knew they could get away with it have the same negative views of women as do rapists. The latter just hold them in extreme form. And since there are many nonoffending males who are hostile towards, or fearful of, women, the status of a man's relationship with his mother in childhood is probably of limited value in distinguishing sex offenders.

In exercising power over women, rapists frequently go beyond aggression and hostility and attempt to degrade their victims. While working as a doctoral student at the Kingston clinic, Juliet Darke reviewed the police reports and victim impact statements on sixty-eight sexual assaults. Her purpose was to determine how many of the rapists clearly intended to humiliate their victims, regardless of their other motives. While all rape victims feel degraded—and no doubt this is a source of pleasure for most rapists—

Darke accepted only proof that the rapists had an explicit intent to humiliate. She found such evidence in sixty-three percent of the cases. Some offenders verbally debased their victims. Others sodomized the women, ejaculated or urinated on their faces, or thrust objects into their vaginas or anuses.

Rapists will often articulate their intent to humiliate their victims. In their book *Why Men Rape*, Sylvia Levine and Joseph Koenig quote one rapist as saying, "I think the reason we used to do this [gang rape] was because I like to lower the chicks to me, that's the way I used to think that I was lowering them and making them look cheap . . . and making them look like dirty tramps . . . she was really humiliated; she was really put down."

Child molesters also enjoy the power they have over their victims, although they are not so often intent on humiliating them. Since children are trained to be obedient to adults, molesting them makes inadequate men feel in control in a way they rarely experience otherwise.

Peter, a middle-aged farmer who molested his own two daughters from the time they were six years of age until they were twelve, said he enjoyed ordering the girls to do sexual things to him and to each other. He viewed his children as his property, with whom he could do as he pleased. In fact, he admitted, the feeling of being in control of them was even more pleasurable than the sex. Peter's masturbatory fantasies also focused on power, and he liked to delay ejaculation as long as possible to prolong the pleasure of being in charge.

Child molesters typically do not seem to express hostility in their offences, but there are exceptions. Jim was a tall, attractive truck driver with an adolescent demeanour who liked to talk in CB lingo. He had a long history of sexually assaulting prepubescent girls, one as young as three years of age. He said he was unable to satisfy his sexual urges with adult women because he was repulsed by their mature sexual features. His wife had been sixteen when he married her and looked about twelve. When she grew older, he lost interest in her and satisfied his sexual needs by going back to very young girls.

On one occasion, however, Jim uncharacteristically molested his wife's thirteen-year-old sister, who was physically mature. He explained to his therapist that he and his wife had been out to dinner that evening and had had a heated argument about his offence history. He said he was feeling very angry towards his wife when he took home her sister, who had been baby-sitting their children. He was clear about why he had assaulted the teenager during the trip: "I wanted to hurt my wife." But, the therapist pointed out, he had told the girl to keep silent about the incident and had even threatened her to ensure she did not tell his wife. "Yes," Jim said, "but my revenge would have been all the sweeter if my wife didn't find out. I would have secretly hurt her and that is worse when you don't know."

Like all sex offenders, Jim had a number of motives for his assaults, and the motives changed from one attack to another. In addition to wanting to hurt his wife, he was motivated by the degree of admiration that he perceived in children when he gave them attention, including sexual attention, which he never got from adults.

Like Robert Noyes, many child molesters seek out positions where they will have ready access to children and be in a position of power over them. They become teachers, scout masters, sports coaches or baby-sitters, for example. In some cases, this involves longterm planning. A psychiatrist who treats sex offenders in New York State tells the story of a pediatrician who decided when he was only eighteen years old to enter medical school and become a child specialist so he would have a ready supply of victims. He was eventually convicted after many years when he masturbated a number of children in front of their parents, assuring them that he was simply making sure "all the apparatus worked." One can only wonder how aware of their proclivities were the Newfoundland priests recently convicted of sexual abuse, when they entered the seminary.

Incest offenders, in particular, use their positions of power over children. Of those followed by the Kingston clinic over the past fifteen years, all of the men who reoffended—twenty-two percent of an untreated group and eight percent of a treated group—did so after leaving their own families and finding another woman with children of the age and gender they preferred.

Both the rape of a woman and the sexual assault of a child involve an imbalance of power with the offender being dominant. However, the most obvious difference is that rape is always explicitly coercive, whereas child molesters typically try persuasive tactics. They may befriend their victims long in advance of their sexual advances, taking them on special outings, for example, or offering them money or candy. Similarly, incest offenders may give their abused children liberties they would not otherwise get. Although some incest offenders physically abuse their children, independent of the sexual abuse, and some child molesters are sadistic, generally they use violence only when cajolery fails or the child threatens to report them.

Many sex offenders—both rapists and child molesters—suffer from a lack of intimacy and sense of social alienation. These traits are not always easy to detect. Some sex offenders are loners who have no friends or only superficial acquaintances. Others are married or involved in relationships, although they are usually perceived by their partners or friends to be distant. The second group may superficially fulfil the outward expectations of a relationship but tend to avoid the responsibilities. Sometimes this avoidance takes the form of excessive pandering to the needs of others outside the relationship. One child molester treated at the Kingston clinic, for example, spent an astonishing amount of time in church and community activities. His family resented his absence from the home, but his neighbours thought he was an ideal husband and citizen. In therapy, the offender reported that he was unhappy in his marriage and felt unfulfilled when he had sex with his wife. She was unaware of his unhappiness, however, and said that for the most part, their life together was good, although she commented that "he did not seem to be there" when they made love.

Why some men fail to develop a capacity for intimacy is not well understood, but it is clear that men generally have more problems in this regard than do women. Males tend not to have the type of close relationships that females forge with their friends and can easily transfer to their partners. No doubt this is a result of the way in which society as a whole socializes boys and girls. It is something that should be changed.

A lack of intimacy in a person's life produces emotional loneliness. For the majority of rapists, this in turn leads to aggressive and assaultive behaviour. Some, however, have told their therapists, as absurd as it may seem, that they secretly hoped their victims would fall in love with them.

Child molesters like Robert Noyes are also trying to fulfil their need for intimacy by assaulting children, and often distort their crimes to portray them as romantic incidents, even when the child was clearly frightened. Other child molesters see themselves as benevolent teachers. Ron told his therapist he was doing his victims a favour by introducing them to sex. He did not see any inconsistency in this view and the fact that several of the young girls he molested cried as he had sex with them. Children, Ron said, often cry when you are teaching them the proper way to behave.

Dan's case illustrates how sex offenders can have completely skewed notions of their behaviour. A thirty-nine-year-old security officer, he was a regular church-goer who described himself as devoted to the Lord and to his wife and daughter. He sought out a psychologist at his wife's insistence after several years of marriage. She said he had become withdrawn, aloof, disinterested in sex with her and, on the rare occasions on which he tried, often impotent.

During the course of therapy, Dan revealed that he had been secretly watching his twelve-year-old daughter take showers through the glass above the bathroom door and surreptitiously masturbating. He said he had not been able to bring himself to reveal his thoughts and feelings to anyone for fear of rejection. When he peeped at his daughter, he said he imagined that she adored him and admired his strength and knowledge. When he then masturbated, it made him feel close to her. Dan had no desire to turn his fantasy into reality; he said he enjoyed the intimacy but did not want to be any closer.

Sex offenders are frequently driven to commit their crimes out of a feeling of deprivation, not necessarily sexual. Dan felt he deserved to enjoy himself by secretly watching his daughter bathe because he had done so much for his family. His model behaviour as a husband and father, he said, deserved a proper reward—that is, sexual satisfaction—which he could not get any other way.

Individuals who try to fulfil the roles of worker, provider, parent, and spouse in an ideal manner typically feel that their efforts are not sufficiently rewarded. Although friends and often their own families express admiration and appreciation for their behaviour, this proves not to be enough, particularly after years of effort. Consequently, they experience an almost continuous state of deprivation. For sex offenders in this category, this feeling leads them to seek out women to rape or children to molest. Not surprisingly, since they feel that their labours have not been rewarded, they also feel considerable resentment and hostility, and this induces a need for revenge. For these men, sexually assaulting a woman or a child reduces their sense of deprivation, while at the same time satisfying their need to strike back at women in particular or at the world in general for being so unfair to them.

It is unlikely that we will ever be able to identify a single motive for sex offending. All men have sexual desires. All men wish to have power. All men need intimacy. And most men feel deprived at one time or another. The satisfaction of these needs may never be complete, and their frustration certainly does not inevitably result in sexual crimes. The lifelong path that leads a man to become a sex offender is complex and unique, as is the course that allows a man to live offence free.

Human behaviour can never be explained in terms of just one or two motives. A man may become a physician because he enjoys helping people, because he reveres life and health, because he wants to comprehend his own body, or because he enjoys learning. It may be that he wants prestige, wants to demonstrate to himself and his family that he is capable, enjoys the power involved in making life-and-death decisions, or desires a high standard of living. No doubt, to some degree, all of these motives—some admirable, others crass—play a part in the decision to become a doctor. The same is true for all behaviour; it is caused by many factors.

To complicate things further, the order of motives changes from time to time. For instance, altruistic motives may be preeminent in a physician's original decision to enter medical school. But after years of training, intense study, and low income, the desire to earn a good salary may be dominant. So it is with sex offenders. On one occasion, a rapist may feel frustrated and helpless in everyday life and want to satisfy his power needs. Another day, he may be strongly aroused sexually, perhaps as a result of viewing pornography, and sexual desire may be his strongest motive for offending. The same is true of child molesters. If they have been treated contemptuously by another adult, for example, their need to be in control may be greater than their need for sexual satisfaction. Or they may offend out of habit, because they are intoxicated or bored or simply because the opportunity arises.

The constantly changing nature and order of motives is as typical of sex offenders as it is of any other human behaviour. Jeff, an incest offender, always took advantage of the fact that his wife was away from the house on Friday nights to have sex with their twelve-year-old daughter. After several interviews at the Kingston clinic, he told a psychologist, "You are going to think I am weird, but you know, I often had sex with my daughter when I wasn't even horny. I don't know why, but it is true."

Jeff was not the first sex offender to make this admission. Sometimes, sexual practices, whether deviant or normal, become routine and are practised as much out of habit as out of immediate desire. Some men, offenders or not, feel that they must take advantage of every opportunity for sex even if they are not feeling particularly aroused because such opportunities may occur infrequently.

While sex offenders have drives that are not dissimilar from those of the rest of us, they have found quite inappropriate ways to satisfy their desires. This is what differentiates them from other men. Through an accident of history, they became vulnerable to experiences and temptations that nonoffending men either have not had or did not respond to, and they learned to express their needs in unacceptable ways.

Various clinicians working with sex offenders have developed theories about the causes of their behaviour. So have some academics who have little or no direct experience with these men or their victims. Most theories seem to fit with our knowledge of at least one offender or to describe one of the motives underlying many offences. There is probably a grain of truth in all theories on sex offenders, but none of them does justice to the complexity of motives involved, and all of them fail to take account of the very obvious fact that the motives for any human behaviour change over time. One of these theories is the sociobiologists' viewpoint on rape. Though this theory has the most repugnant social implications, it has won many adherents in the Western world over the past decade, particularly among those who hold traditional patriarchal views of human society. Indeed, one of the foremost advocates of sociobiology, Edward Wilson, holds that patriarchy is an inevitable outcome of evolutionary processes, and that attempts to make our world more gender-equal are doomed to crash on the rocks of our genetic heritage.

Sociobiologists offer what amounts to an evolutionary justification for rape. According to this perspective, rape is simply one way for males cut off from socially acceptable access to female sexual partners to ensure that their genetic endowment is passed on to another generation. To suggest, however, that rapists are driven by some genetic force beyond their control is untenable.

If men only raped to fulfil their need to pass on their genes (as opposed to fulfilling sexual urges, which all human beings possess and can satisfy in non-violent ways, such as masturbation), then males would rape whenever they were deprived of a ready consenting partner. Yet anthropologists have found wide discrepancies in the frequency of rape across human societies. Furthermore, even within any one society, the tendency by males to rape varies considerably. That relatively few men rape (though, almost certainly more than are ever reported and caught), and that these men rape only under conditions where they are likely to get away with it, indicates that this behaviour is very much learned, not genetically inherited. And since the crime itself typically involves a range of abusive and degrading behaviours that go far beyond what is necessary to overpower a victim, as well as numerous sexual acts that cannot lead to impregnation, the sociobiologists' account will not help us to understand the genesis of rape.

This theory also ignores the sexual abuse of children, perhaps because such abuse cannot be motivated, however unconsciously, by a desire to impregnate a woman and thereby ensure the survival of a male's genes.

While the human propensity for simplicity has been helpful throughout history in solving many problems, in this case, it has obscured our understanding and encouraged us to develop a false image of sex offenders. This, in turn, has helped foster fallacious attitudes about the nature and extent of sexual crimes— myths that, as we will see, allow so many sex offenders to avoid punishment and offend with impunity.

6

Shattering the Myths

AFTER FOURTEEN YEARS of working with the victims of rape and incest, Pam Benson is still shocked. Not by the extent of sexual crimes—which her waiting list of patients has long demonstrated—and, after this many years, usually not even by the degree of horror and torture that her most abused patients reveal to her.

What increasingly shocks and depresses the Kingston therapist is that most people don't seem to care.

Benson works in the family medicine centre at a general hospital just two miles from Kingston Penitentiary. Her office is spacious and restful. The floor is covered by an Indian-style rug. A framed art poster adorns one wall. Over her desk is a billboard that includes family photographs and postcards of lakeside scenes. On top of a round coffee table, between two armchairs, are a lavishly illustrated gardening maga-

zine, a bouquet of dried heather, and a purple sparkle-
filled wand. In this tranquil sanctuary, patients slowly
reveal tales of sexual assault, memories of which they
have often suppressed for years.

Benson herself has a calm demeanour. But at the
same time, she is passionate about her work and forth-
right in her views. She doesn't skirt uncomfortable
issues, and she doesn't tread lightly where she sees
inequality or injustice.

"It is almost unbelievable the degree of torture and
abuse and perversion that goes on," she says during a
break on a warm summer's morning. "I've had patients
who were dangled out of moving vehicles, hung from
the ceiling, whipped, had objects shoved into their
vaginas. Women who as children were subjected to
abortions when they didn't even know what was going
on, who were cut and burned..."

It saddens her. But it also makes her angry. "Part of
what allows this to continue is the social attitudes we
have towards sexual assault. We deny it. We downplay
it. We say it really isn't so important. We give a guy
forty-five days that he can serve on weekends so he can
still go to work. We don't give a guy forty-five days that
he can serve on weekends if he breaks into someone's
house, but if he rapes a woman...

"That's the crazy-making part of it—the social response. Because it goes on in a context of, at the very
least, society turning a blind eye to it, and at the most,
actively supporting it through pornography and violence in the media."

Chief among the myths fostering society's attitudes
is the notion that sexual crimes are not widespread.
Benson and other counsellors on the front lines of the
unbridled epidemic of sexual assault know better than
anyone that incarcerated sex offenders are only a small
proportion of the men committing sex crimes in Canada. Most sexual assaults are never even reported. And

of those that are, very few result in a conviction. The Canadian government does not keep statistics on the conviction rates for sexual crimes, but the Federal Bureau of Investigation has calculated that over half of the rape cases in the U.S. that actually reach the courts are dismissed.

Sex offenders who kill or mutilate their victims usually get caught. So do many sex offenders who assault strangers and fit society's stereotypical image of a rapist or child molester. These men are often from a lower socioeconomic background, which in turn means they cannot afford the best legal representation, decreasing their chances of acquittal. But they are the minority. The rest, including those from middle- and upper-class backgrounds and those who sexually assault members of their own families or their dates, often go free. Their victims, fearful of retaliation, or the ordeal of testifying, or simply of not being believed, keep the crimes secret; or members of the criminal justice system, like the rest of society, frequently deny both the extent and the nature of sexual offences and dismiss the charges.

Based on numerous surveys that asked women about their experiences of sexual assault, academics estimate that only ten to twenty percent of victims notify the police. The federal solicitor-general's department says that forty percent do.

In 1988, according to Statistics Canada, the police received 29,111 reports of sexual assault. Even using the government's conservative estimate that these reports reflect forty percent of assaults actually committed, this means there were actually 72,777 incidents of sexual assault that year—200 a day. One every seven minutes.

The prevalence of sexual assault has been demonstrated by numerous scientific studies. In 1984, the Badgley parliamentary committee on sexual offences against children and youths reported that one in four females and one in eight males in Canada are sexually abused—eighty percent before the age of twenty-one. Four years earlier, a study of women from all parts of Winnipeg, Manitoba, revealed that twenty-seven percent had been sexually assaulted. A 1988 survey of undergraduate female students at Winnipeg's University of Manitoba, who were on average 19.7 years old, showed that thirty-nine percent had been victims of forced sexual activity; sixteen percent had been victims of rape or attempted rape.

Despite these figures, the myth that sexual assault against women and children is an isolated occurrence continues, nurturing society's apathy toward sex crimes. There is also a belief, at least with respect to adults, that "nice" people are not sexually assaulted and that victims somehow provoke the attacks.

James Check, a professor of psychology at York University in Toronto, surveyed 436 men in that city in 1985, asking them about their attitudes to rape. The respondents, who came from a wide range of educational and social backgrounds, ranged in age from eighteen to seventy-eight. Thirty-four percent of them believed that a quarter or more of reported rapes were "merely invented by women who discover they are pregnant and want to protect their own reputation." Forty-five percent of the men said that a quarter or more of women who report being raped are lying because they are angry and want to get back at the man they accuse. Eleven percent agreed with the statement, "Many women have an unconscious wish to be raped, and may then unconsciously set up a situation in which they are likely to be attacked." Twenty percent accepted the assertion, "One reason that women falsely report a rape is that they frequently have a need to call attention to themselves."

Even young children are sometimes impugned. In

late 1989, a Vancouver judge gave a suspended sentence to a man who admitted to sexually assaulting a three-year-old girl; the judge accepted defence assertions that the victim had been "sexually aggressive."

Men are not alone in blaming the victims of sexual crimes. A 1980 poll conducted in Minnesota by Martha Burt, a psychologist at the Urban Institute in Washington, D.C., found that more than half of 598 male and female residents surveyed agreed with such statements as, "In the majority of rapes, the victim was promiscuous or had a bad reputation." A 1987 study at the University of Missouri studied the attitudes of seventy-six female undergraduates towards date rape. Researchers discovered that as the observers' feelings of susceptibility of the victim's situation increased, they were more likely to blame the victim. In other words, threatened by the prospect of their own vulnerability, the women viewed the victim as being more blameworthy or incompetent than themselves. This was true even if the observer herself had previously been sexually assaulted.

One generous interpretation of this blame-the-victim attitude has been proposed by M.J. Lerner, an American psychologist. He postulates that people want to believe that good things happen to good people and bad things happen to bad people. In order to maintain their conviction that the world is a fair place, people view the victim of a misfortune as causing his or her own troubles or as being someone who deserves to suffer.

Just as sex offenders come from all walks of life, however, so, too, can any woman or child become a victim of sexual assault. There is no age, social class, ethnic group, religion, lifestyle, attire, occupation, or location that protects them. Sex offenders have raped infants and women in their nineties. They have sexually assaulted women and children on the street in broad daylight; and they have broken into homes where women had been sleeping and attacked them.

In 1989, a middle-aged woman was asleep in her Toronto apartment when a man in his early twenties climbed two balconies and broke in. After using a telephone cord to tie her hands and a cord from an iron to bind her feet, he raped her and left. It took her five hours to free herself.

The same year, another young man broke into a Winnipeg home and sexually assaulted a terminally-ill seventy-nine year old woman.

For sex offenders who attack strangers, sexual assault is often a random crime; they do not care who their victims are. Other offenders assail members of their immediate families—relatives, lovers, friends, and casual acquaintances.

The presumed nature of these assaults constitutes another common misconception supporting society's repudiation of sexual assault: people like to believe that rape is, typically, vaginal intercourse without consent, and crimes against children merely fondling. So tenaciously do Canadians hang on to this notion that Crown attorneys have admitted privately to counselling rape victims not to reveal in court everything that happened during a sexual assault because it will weaken the chances of a conviction. While the jury might believe that an accused man, dressed in a suit, speaking politely and articulately, and perhaps expressing remorse, might have forced a woman to have vaginal intercourse, it will have great difficulty believing that he committed other more disgusting acts. Thus, the myth is perpetuated.

The reality is far different. Sexual assaults against children over the age of ten almost always involve some form of intercourse. And assaults against adult women usually involve a wide range of sexual behaviours and often last for hours.

When Lonnie Allan Mowers finally abandoned the three Oakville, Ontario, teenage girls that he abducted in 1985, for example, he had repeatedly raped and sodomized each of them and had forced each to fellate him twice. The ordeal lasted seventeen hours.

Studies by Nicholas Groth, the American psychologist, explain how such a marathon of sexual assault is possible. He has found that at the time of their crimes, one-third of rapists suffer some form of sexual dysfunction: impotence, premature ejaculation, or retarded ejaculation. He cites the case of a man who broke into a house when a woman, her husband, and two children were home. The man locked the husband and children in a closet and then sexually assaulted the woman seven times in a series of sexual acts including vaginal intercourse, sodomy, and fellatio. One assault lasted a full half hour. A medical examination of the victim revealed no semen.

Similarly, the sexual abuse of children encompasses a variety of sexual behaviours ranging from an offender exposing himself or masturbating in front of a child, to mutual masturbation or fondling, to rape. Canadians learned, through the judicial inquiry into Newfoundland's justice system in the fall of 1989, that all of these acts had been perpetrated against the boys at Mount Cashel orphanage in St. John's during the early 1970s. Former residents testified that they had been fondled in the shower, in the swimming pool, and in their beds at night. They had been forced to put their hands down their assailants' pants and to fellate them. A few had also been sodomized.

In a survey of the crimes committed by convicted child molesters referred to a Massachusetts forensic mental health clinic for evaluation, Groth found that thirty-nine percent were confined to fondling or masturbation; thirty-one percent involved oral, anal, or vaginal penetration; and thirteen percent included both. No data were available for seventeen percent of the study population.

Even infants are not safe from child molesters

outside or inside their own homes. A study of incest at Boston City Hospital's pediatric walk-in clinic showed that nearly twenty-seven percent of victims were aged one to five. Roughly twenty-five percent were six to nine years of age; thirty-two percent, ten to thirteen; and sixteen percent, fourteen to sixteen.

Occasionally the assaults are incredibly sadistic. A Kingston father sodomized his two-year-old son so forcefully in 1988 that the child had to undergo surgery and be fitted with a colostomy bag.

Although children are not usually expected to fight off their assailants, when adults do not, their behaviour is often interpreted as consent. A defence attorney told a jury at a 1988 rape trial in Thompson, Manitoba, that the sixteen year old victim would have lashed out at the man she said sexually assaulted her if she really didn't want to go to bed with him. "Her resistance consisted, she says, of pushing him away and telling him to leave her alone. There was no ripped clothing. She didn't bite, scratch, or hit him. But this is the type of behaviour that should be expected of someone having forcible sex inflicted on them."

The remark reveals the extent to which even some professionals (who interact with victims and their assailants and should know better) accept the myths about rape. The fact is that when rapists do not use weapons in the commission of their offences, they sometimes threaten to kill their victims if they do not comply. Even if no verbal threats are made, the inherent violence of the rape itself is terrifying. Many victims have described how they froze when suddenly attacked, likening their experience to that of a rabbit on the highway who sits paralyzed in front of an oncoming car, transfixed by headlights.

In addition to the sexual assault itself, however, victims of all ages are commonly subjected to physical abuse. A 1979 study by the Kingston Sexual Behaviour

Clinic of 150 incarcerated sex offenders showed that seventy-one percent of rapists and fifty-eight percent of child molesters used force beyond what was necessary to commit their crimes. Half of these victims required treatment for their injuries.

Groth says this type of rapist "attacks his victim, grabbing her, striking her, knocking her to the ground, beating her, tearing her clothes, and raping her. He may use a blitz style of attack, a violent surprise offensive, in which the victim is caught completely off guard. Or he may use a confidence-style approach to gain access to the victim and then launch a sudden, overpowering attack. In the former situation, the offender approaches the victim directly by hitting her. In the latter situation, victims often relate that at first the assailant seemed pleasant enough, but that at some point, he changed. Suddenly and without warning, he became mean and angry."

Victims who do fight back have no guarantee that they will ward off an attack. They might even worsen the situation. A 1986 study of Loyola University of Chicago showed that in potential rape incidents involving strangers, forceful resistance was related to higher risk of attack and bodily harm with no apparent reduction in the risk of rape. The researchers based their analysis on data from the U.S. National Crime Survey, which interviews about 21,000 Americans every month on their experiences with crime.

What deters one assailant may only encourage another, according to Groth. He quotes one offender as saying, "When my victim screamed, I ran like hell." But another told him, "When my victim screamed, I cut her throat."

While society tends to criticize women who do not aggressively resist attack, its greatest censure is for victims who know their assailants. They are even more likely than women and children who are sexually assaulted by strangers to be blamed for the crimes or disbelieved entirely. This is little recognition of the abuse of trust and the frequent abuse of power involved in such crimes or of the devastating and long-lasting effects these offences can have on the victims.

"As a child," says Benson, "you trust the adults who are supposed to look after you. As an adult, you trust your friends. You don't go out with someone you don't trust. If they then hurt you, it's a profound betrayal of your trust." Rev. Kevin Molloy, the Roman Catholic Church's spokesperson in Newfoundland, agrees: "If the person you trust the most hurts you like this, how can you trust anyone?"

David Finkelhor, a psychologist at the University of New Hampshire, points out in a 1979 paper on the ethics of sexual assault that children can never be considered to have agreed to sex with an adult. "For true consent to occur," he writes, "two conditions must prevail. A person must know what it is that he or she is consenting to and a person must be free to say yes or no."

The former charges of Mount Cashel orphanage testified at the judicial inquiry that they were regularly subjected to severe physical abuse. One was taken into a closet and beaten with a belt until he bled as a result of misplacing a library card; another had a crutch broken over his back and was then deliberately scalded after he was late for a dance; others were punched in the face and beaten with hockey sticks, broom handles, and wooden mallets. There was an unspoken agreement, however, according to John MacIsaac, a past resident: "If you went along with the sexual acts, the physical beatings weren't going to happen as much."

An Ottawa court was told in 1988 that a thirty-seven year old father who sexually assaulted his daughter for five years from the time she was eight years old had forced the young girl to sign a contract to perform sexual acts until 1991. The one-page typewritten pact promised rewards for compliance and punishments for failure to comply.

Even when the behaviour of an incest perpetrator or a pedophile is gentle and cajoling at the onset, it often accelerates over time both in terms of the sexual activity and the coercion that accompanies it. So, too, can the deviant proclivities of so-called nuisance sex offenders accelerate; for example, Warren, described in Chapter 4, began his offence career by exposing his genitals but eventually molested a child and viciously raped a psychiatric patient.

While the attitudes of society in general prevent most victims from reporting sexual crimes, the assimilation of these biases by many professionals, including members of the criminal justice system, too often serves to dismiss or even punish those victims who do complain. Ignorance about the true nature of sex crimes and the devastating effects they can cause has led to countless incidents of associates covering up for one another, of authorities failing to pursue allegations of sexual assault, and of judges downplaying the severity of the crimes that do make it to court.

7

Turning a Blind Eye

IN DECEMBER 1975, a police investigation began into allegations of physical and sexual abuse at Mount Cashel orphanage in St. John's, Newfoundland. Twenty-six boys had complained. Two members of the Christian Brothers, the Roman Catholic lay order that ran the ninety year old orphanage, had confessed. Yet a week later, according to the investigating officers, the chief of police abruptly ordered them to forget the case. After fourteen years, the victims found out why. The provincial superior of the Christian Brothers had made a deal with Newfoundland's deputy attorney-general and the police chief: the offenders would be sent out of the province, and the matter would be dropped.

A year after the bargain was struck, the deputy attorney-general, Vincent McCarthy, returned the police reports on the discontinued investigation to the incoming chief of the Royal Newfoundland Constabulary with the instruction: "In view of the action taken by the Christian Brothers, further police action is unwarranted in this matter."

Rumours of a cover-up at Mount Cashel had been circulating around St. John's since 1972. The scandal reached a peak in 1989 after nine members of the Christian Brothers were charged with sexual assault. The uproar was intensified by the fact that two priests had recently been convicted of molesting altar boys in small fishing villages near the city; the incidents dated as far back as seventeen years in the case of one priest, seven years in the other. People across the country demanded to know how all this abuse could have gone on so long without any criminal charges being laid. The Church responded by appointing a five-member task force to look into the matter; the government announced a more wide-ranging inquiry into the province's justice system.

Several weeks after the provincial inquiry began in September 1989, the ugly truth about the 1975 Mount Cashel investigation began to emerge. There had indeed been collusion. But that was not all. Veronica Strickland, a former welfare recipient who had three sons living in the orphanage in the mid-1970s, testified that shortly after the investigation was stopped, she told Anthony Murphy, the province's minister of social services, that she was going to give the media tape-recorded conversations in which boys from Mount Cashel talked about their abuse. She said Murphy told her she would never be reunited with her children if she did; he said his department had a psychiatric report on her that could be used to prove she was an incompetent parent. The minister further suggested, Strickland alleged, that she leave the province. She did; she was reunited with her children a year and a half later in Nova Scotia. (Murphy told the inquiry several months later that he

knew nothing about the investigation at Mount Cashel
in 1975.)

Another woman, Carol Baird, whose sons were
temporarily placed in the orphanage in the mid-1970s,
told the inquiry that she did tell the press what was
happening there. But she later asked the newspaper
not to publish her story for fear of antagonizing the
police, who had told her not to discuss the issue with
reporters.

The former news editor of the St. John's *Evening
Telegram* testified that the newspaper's publisher refused, after the offending brothers had left the province, to run an article about the abuse because he felt it
could do more harm that good.

It was partly the threat of publicity that had launched
the original investigation. Chesley Riche, a mainte-
nance man at the orphanage, testified that when he
complained about the abuse in December 1975 to
Frank Simms, the provincial director of child welfare,
"the man told me: 'The Catholic Church is on a pedestal. We can't touch them.' I said, 'You do something, or
I'll put you and your pedestal on the front page of the
Telegram.'"

The conversation took place after Riche helped
Shane Earle, a nine-year-old resident who had been
severely beaten with a belt for losing his library card,
go to his mother's apartment. Riche notified the police
of the abuse; so did the doctor who examined the boy
the following day. In 1989, Earle told his story to the
media himself, which led to charges finally being laid
against the brothers.

The police suspected before 1975 that residents at
Mount Cashel were being beaten and sexually assaulted,
a former social worker told the 1989 inquiry. A past
resident corroborated her testimony, while shedding
light on the insensitivity of the investigators. John
MacIsaac said he was asked by the police in 1972

whether he had ever been touched or beaten by the brothers: "But the brother who was abusing me was standing behind me . . . so I flatly denied it."

Other former residents, many of them sobbing as they related their experiences at the orphanage, said they had told relatives, teachers, social workers, police officers, and in one case, even politicians what was happening to them. Nobody did anything. When he told an older relative, Gerald Nash said, "her response was, 'That doesn't happen with Christian Brothers.'" A St. John's high school teacher said a resident of the orphanage came to him in tears in 1974 after he had been badly beaten by one of the brothers for calling him a "queer." The man said he showed the boy's bruises to his homeroom teacher; "she just shrugged her shoulders and said something like, 'What do you want me to do about it?'" He said he was still haunted by images of the battered boy and the fact that he, too, failed to get help.

Even as the church and government inquiries were beginning in 1989, the attitudes that had conspired to keep the crimes at Mount Cashel silent fourteen years earlier were still very much in evidence. Colin Campbell, a Newfoundland bishop, wrote in a newspaper column on May 17, 1989: "If the victims were adolescents, why did they go back to the same situation once there had been one pass or suggestion? Were they cooperating in the matter or were they true victims?" The bishop commented later to a reporter, "What I'm suggesting is that maybe some—a few, a few of them, many of them, who knows—had some kind of inkling that this was wrong and could have said, 'No, thank you very much.'"

Alphonsus Penney, the archbishop of St. John's, further enraged Catholics across the province by refusing to condemn publicly the actions of the two priests, James Hickey and John Corrigan, who had been sent to prison for five years for sexually assaulting altar boys. In the spring of 1989, the archbishop announced the formation of the task force. Otherwise, he remained silent about the matter, refusing media requests for interviews. When the task force held its three meetings that summer, the archbishop went on a spiritual retreat.

Former residents of Mount Cashel spoke poignantly at the government inquiry about the sense of betrayal they still felt. When the police investigation began in 1975, former resident Dereck O'Brien told the inquiry, "We said, 'Now something is finally going to happen' —we felt safe." When it was halted, Shane Earle testified: "It felt like they shut the door on us and society really didn't care what happened to the kids at Mount Cashel."

While the reverence surrounding members of the Catholic Church in Newfoundland contributed to the victimization of the orphanage residents, many people feel that the attitudes and teachings of the Church itself are also partly to blame. By excluding women from the priesthood and, indeed, any decision-making role in the Church, and by requiring priests to be celibate, its doctrine has promoted a negative view of both women and sex. The neophyte priest who struggles to suppress his natural sexual inclinations and then gives in and masturbates must feel he has failed. (Anyone who has a lapse while trying to resist a strong temptation experiences a sense of failure that makes it even harder to resist temptation in the future.) If he interprets such lapses as an indication that, unlike his brethren, he is unable to control himself, he may finally give in to the impulse to have sex with another person. Given the Church's view of women, however, it is unlikely he will seek out an adult female. Sex with boys, to whom he will also have readier access, may not seem as bad to him as sex with a woman and certainly will not lead to pregnancy.

However quintessential its patriarchy, the Catholic

Church is not alone in the perpetuation of attitudes that tolerate sexual assault. There are countless recent examples of professionals outside the clergy who exploit the widespread denial of the extent and nature of sexual crimes in order to assault women and children with impunity.

Students at a high school in Ashcroft, British Columbia, for instance, must have felt the same sense of abandonment as the boys at Mount Cashel when they complained to their parents in the mid-1980s about being sexually molested by their principal. The allegations against the handsome, intelligent, charming Robert Noyes were not believed.

Noyes was finally arrested in 1985. The following January, he pleaded guilty to sexually assaulting nineteen children over a fifteen-year period. Most were between the ages of nine and eleven; all but one were boys. Evidence at his sentencing hearing uncovered the same attitudes that protected the Christian Brothers for so many years.

Noyes had been caught molesting children on many occasions dating back to 1968. No one called the police. The first time he was caught, he was an education student at the University of British Columbia; the assault occurred on a camping trip. Two years later, Noyes took a year off school and was employed by the Children's Aid Society as a supervisor at a Vancouver centre for troubled children. A young boy ran out of the dormitory screaming that Noyes had tried to rape him. Noyes was fired.

Within a week, Noyes was working at a boys' camp in Burnaby, near Vancouver. Again, his molestation of young boys was discovered; he was asked to resign. Back at university in 1971, he worked as a volunteer at a boys' club; this time, his sexual behaviour resulted in the threat of a police charge, but no more. He was barred from the club.

In 1978, when Noyes was teaching elementary school, two mothers of young students complained to the principal that Noyes was molesting their sons. The women testified at his 1986 sentencing hearing that the principal had talked them out of calling the police, promising that Noyes would never teach again. The principal informed the school superintendent. Noyes went on sick leave and later resigned.

In 1982, Noyes was a teacher at another elementary school when a mother reported to the principal that he was having her son sit on his lap. The principal suggested she speak to Noyes herself. She did. She told the court four years later that Noyes implied her son was the one with the sexual problem and the one making the advances.

By 1985, Noyes was principal of the high school in Ashcroft. When a girl who had been abused before was transferred to the school, she told a social worker about her trip to the principal's office. This time, the police were called and Noyes was finally charged. In June 1986, Noyes was designated a dangerous offender and sentenced to an indefinite term in prison.

The same year, another British Columbia teacher, Peter Reid, was sentenced to three years in prison for sexually assaulting young boys and girls at a youth drop-in centre he operated in his home near Port McNeil. A presentence report stated that Reid had been suspended from teaching at a high school in Ontario for being involved with one nineteen-year-old student and for using drugs with other students. There was no mention of the suspension on his job record. In fact, the Ontario school had given him a positive evaluation.

In 1987, a minor controversy erupted in Toronto following a newspaper report of a male teacher who was first transferred from one school to another and then asked to resign after parents and students wrote a total of twenty-eight letters complaining about his behaviour. The letters charged that the teacher gave the students strange hugs, rubbed and poked them, put his hand under their shirts, and chased the girls around the classroom trying to spray their blouses with water. Police and children's aid agencies had been called in but the police decided there was not enough evidence to lay charges. The newspaper reported that the teacher was subsequently hired by a school in another city borough; officials there did not check with the board of education in the first borough because the teacher had given them letters of recommendation from two of his former principals.

In October 1988, the chief superintendent of the Winnipeg School Division defended to the media the division's earlier decision not to notify the police about allegations of a teacher's criminal conduct. Two years before, parents and students had signed complaints attesting that a high school teacher gave liquor to underage female students at parties in his home and had the girls stay overnight with him. The teacher was transferred to a school for children with emotional problems. He resigned from that job in June 1988, and in July, he was charged with sexual assault and having sex with a girl under the age of sixteen. The superintendent told reporters in October: "We acted properly and dealt with the matter as we saw fit."

The same month, a principal at a Winnipeg private school was under fire for doing nothing after three female students wrote him letters detailing physical and sexual assaults against them by a male classmate. The matter was eventually brought to light after the mother of one of the students witnessed a sexual assault on her fifteen-year-old daughter. The male student was subsequently charged. When the case was brought to the attention of the attorney-general's department, a prosecutor who reviewed the circumstances said the principal had done nothing illegal! Legislation required him to report only abuse or suspected abuse perpetrated by a parent or guardian and not assaults by third parties such as classmates.

Not only have society's attitudes about sexual assault shielded sex offenders in professional positions and those associated with their institutions, they have also, as witnessed in Newfoundland, punished some who would expose the offenders. In February 1989, a Cree teacher told the Manitoba aboriginal justice inquiry that she was fired from her job when she informed the principal at a reserve school of sexual assault on her students by two fellow teachers. Ellen Haroun said one teacher was having sex with two juvenile girls in the school, while another was molesting younger students. She said she agreed to be the spokesperson for five teachers who were concerned about the abuse. But when she wrote a letter to the principal regarding the matter, he became angry and demanded that she apologize. When she refused, he dismissed her. "Why is the child's advocate punished, while the perpetrator is allowed to remain at the school?" she asked the inquiry. "Imagine the guilt the children must feel."

Like the rest of society, professional groups are reluctant to confront the issue of sexual crimes. Presented with clear evidence of a sex offender in their midst, institutions tend to think first and foremost about their own reputations, not about the devastating impact on the victims. Then, perhaps to justify their inaction, they often minimize the offences. This is particularly true when those in authority identify with the perpetrators. Sometimes, as Bishop Campbell demonstrated, their denial is expressed in hostility towards the victims.

The ten to forty percent of sexual assault victims who report the crimes face an uphill battle for justice. The first hurdle is getting the police to believe them. In 1985, a study at the University of Manitoba found that police forces in all provinces except Quebec and Saskatchewan subjected some women who complained of being raped to lie detector tests. This occurred despite the fact that the tests are considered by experts to be scientifically unreliable, particularly when applied to individuals who have been traumatized, and their results are not accepted as evidence in court. If a woman refused or failed the test, the researchers reported, the police would consider dropping their investigation. Chief Superintendent Jack White of the RCMP in British Columbia told the Vancouver *Sun* in response to the study that he had authorized the use of the test when a police officer could convince him "he's getting a snow job and we're chasing around looking for something that doesn't exist."

In 1987, a sociologist who reviewed one hundred sexual assault complaints to the Halifax police department reported that the force was reluctant to lay charges for rape unless the woman submitted to a medical examination, even though the law was changed in 1983 and penetration no longer had to be proved. Ronald Hinch, a professor at the University of Guelph in Ontario, added that the force dismissed as unfounded a higher proportion of complaints from women with "bad" sexual or social reputations than from other women. None of the complaints from hitchhikers, for example, concluded with a charge. And police pursued only one of nineteen complaints from women who were intoxicated at the time of the assault. Hinch concluded: "The forces that were once at work to discriminate against women are still there... police are tending to uphold values which hail men for being conquerors."

According to Statistics Canada, police forces dismissed as unfounded a full seventeen percent—4,225 reports—of the sexual assault complaints they received in 1988. The percentage varied widely across the country. Police in the Yukon threw out forty-one percent; in Quebec, which also has the lowest per capita rate of reporting, they rejected seven percent. Authorities in the Northwest Territories and New Brunswick dismissed roughly twenty-five percent; in Alberta, British Columbia, Nova Scotia, Prince Edward Island, Newfoundland, and Saskatchewan, about twenty percent were not pursued. In Ontario, police turned away sixteen percent.

Even when the police do accept the validity of a complaint, they do not necessarily press charges of sexual assault. In May 1989, for example, an Ontario Provincial Police officer investigating an incident in which a fifteen-year-old girl was sexually assaulted and later struck with a car seat-belt strap said the only charges pending alleged common assault. The maximum penalty for sexual assault is ten years; for common assault, two years.

When the police have to track down a sex offender, the charges may just sit on the books, or a victim may have to go to extraordinary lengths to obtain justice. In May 1983, a warrant was issued for the arrest of a fifty-three-year-old truck driver who was accused of sexually assaulting an eight-year-old Calgary girl. For the next four years, he lived in Golden, British Columbia, with his telephone number listed in the directory. Twice during that period, he was stopped by the police for speeding and ticketed. Although the warrant had been routinely filed in the police cross-Canada computer bank, the information was apparently overlooked. When the man was finally picked up in 1987, he offered no resistance. The judge threw the assault charge out of court on the grounds that the man's right to a speedy trial had been violated.

A teacher at a reserve in northern Manitoba told the province's aboriginal justice inquiry in 1988 that the RCMP refused even to investigate an attempted sexual assault against her because the attack was not successful. The woman said she awoke one night the previous summer to find an obviously intoxicated fourteen year old boy standing over her infant's crib holding a bread knife. The youth then pointed the knife at her and told her to undress. She grabbed a baseball bat and hit him over the head; in the ensuing struggle she suffered multiple cuts and bruises, including a facial laceration that required stitches. When the RCMP would not send an officer to the reserve, she photographed the scene of the crime, bagged the assault weapon, wrote a detailed report of what had happened, and caught the next plane to Winnipeg where she handed the evidence to police and identified the youth. She said the teenager remained free for two weeks before he was arrested; then he was sentenced only to probation, even though he had already been on probation for breaking and entering when he forced his way into her home.

Dale Henry, an assistant commissioner with the RCMP, commented afterwards: "In a perfect world, I'd like to see us take immediate action on all cases. But the logistics and staffing in such remote areas of northern Manitoba don't always make this possible, and we need to make priorities."

The evidence suggests that such judgement calls can have tragic consequences. After Clifford Olson was convicted in 1982 of murdering eleven children, whose bodies were found nude and in varying stages of decomposition, the Vancouver *Sun* revealed that Olson had been implicated in at least two previous sex crimes that were not pursued by the police. On August 3, 1978, six weeks after he was released from B.C. Penitentiary on mandatory supervision for the third time (having served four and a half years on the last of a string of convictions for such offences as theft, forgery and fraud), Olson was picked up by the police in Sydney, Nova Scotia, in connection with an indecent assault on a seven year old girl. According to the newspaper, the child had given a detailed description of her attacker, which included the distinctive t-shirt he was wearing when he lured her out of a park and into his hotel. Olson gave his correct name to the two investigating officers and then asked them to wait while he went into his hotel to tell his friends where he was going. He slipped out the back door, leaving his luggage, which contained Polaroid pictures of the victim. A warrant was issued for his arrest. On August 31, Olson was picked up riding a stolen bicycle in Camrose, Alberta, and once again was returned to prison for violating the terms of his release. Authorities in Alberta were unaware of the outstanding warrant in the Maritimes. Olson remained in prison until January 1980 and was released again on mandatory supervision. His release was revoked for a month that spring, but he was let out again in June. On September 7, 1980, his sentence expired; two months later, his first murder victim went missing.

The inspector of criminal investigation for the Sydney police force, William Urquhart, was asked by a reporter in 1982 why his department had not pursued the warrant it had issued in 1978. He replied, "It was an assault case. We weren't going to bring him back all the way from the West Coast for something like that."

The newspaper disclosed that in 1981, Olson was twice charged with sexual assault in the midst of his string of murders. He was charged by police in British Columbia in January in connection with an incident involving a teenage girl. But he was released on April 8 because the police felt the complainant was an unreliable witness. Four months later, he was charged with raping an eighteen year old woman. That charge was dropped after he was arrested for the murder of eleven children.

Many police officers investigating complaints of sexual assault expect that honest victims will always be outwardly upset. A cool demeanour is often interpreted to mean that the woman is lying. Police also tend to doubt victims who do not report the crime immediately, particularly if, in the meantime, the woman did something as routine as going home and making her child's lunch. To address these misconceptions about rape, Toronto's Metro Action Committee on Public Violence Against Women and Children has helped the city's police force set up training programs for officers involved in the investigation of sexual assaults. Patricia Marshall, the committee's executive director, says the program teaches police officers to start with the premise of belief and to understand that women cope with the trauma of sexual assault in many different ways. Unfortunately, such courses are not routinely offered by police forces across Canada.

Even when sexual crimes are reported, accepted as valid by the police, investigated, and referred to the courts as sexual assaults rather than the lesser crime of common assault, they undergo another round of discrimination that often results in dismissal. After a woman has undergone a gruelling medical examination designed to gather evidence, a police interrogation that can last for hours, a preliminary trial in which she may be asked to go over and over the humiliating details of the crime, and then a trial in which she will be cross-examined in front of a room full of strangers, not only about the offence but sometimes also about her personal sexual history, the result is all too often to see her assailant acquitted. (A woman's past sexual experience can no longer be introduced by a defence attorney at a trial unless it is deemed by the judge to fit certain exceptions outlined in law. However, such rulings are not uncommon in date-rape cases and other assaults in which the victim knew her assailant.)

When a man is accused of sexually assaulting an adult, he can use the defence of "honest belief." He may admit, for example, that the woman verbally and physically resisted his sexual advances but claim, nonetheless, that he sincerely believed her protests were feigned and she really wanted to have sex. If the court concludes that the defendant truly mistook the woman's intent, he can be found not guilty.

Regardless of the method of defence, defendants in sexual assault trials have a good chance of going free. Like many police officers, male judges tend to distrust women who do not report sexual assaults immediately and to believe, further, that victims suffer no lasting injuries. A long-term study by the Toronto action committee has also shown that the closer the assailant is to the economic status of the judge, the more tolerant of the sexual assault the judge seems to be. Perhaps the most incredible example of this sentiment can be found in the remarks of Judge Edward Cowart to Ted Bundy when he sentenced him to death for sexually assaulting and killing two members of a Florida State University sorority. Minutes after calling Bundy's crimes "ordeals of extreme savagery," the judge said, "Take care of yourself, young man. I say that to you sincerely. You are a bright young man, and you would have made a good lawyer one day. But you went down the wrong road, partner. I really don't have any animosity towards you. I really want you to know that."

The Toronto action committee has amassed more than 1,000 Canadian sentencing reports that contain similar views, albeit of offenders who are not serial killers. Their data show that judges often blame the victims for provoking sexual assaults, downplay the severity of the crimes, and accept such factors as the offender's family background and employment record as reasons for leniency. "Judges see real rape as a blameless virgin or older woman at home behind locked doors crocheting a flag who is raped when a man breaks in wearing a balaclava," says Patricia Marshall. "Anything else is just bad sex."

The extent to which some judges deny the violent nature of sexual assaults is astonishing. In 1980, an Ontario judge sentenced a man to nine months in jail with a strong recommendation that he be granted temporary absence passes after he was convicted of raping a twenty-year-old nonvirgin; the woman passed out during the assault. The judge commented: "Although he once told her to shut up as she screamed, he never threatened her with harm or otherwise physically assaulted her and did not harm her physically in the act of intercourse. . . . The victim . . . has not suffered any psychological damage."

In 1981, a judge in Ontario sentenced a man to two years less a day for sexually assaulting three young girls and his foster daughter on a weekly basis. The judge explained, "None of the acts involved violence or the use of violence except for one child on one occasion who refused to submit and who was pushed down." In 1986, a man was sent to prison for three years for forcing sexual intercourse with his daughter five hundred times over a nine-year period and attempting to rape his niece; the judge said "there was no physical coercion." In 1988, a judge reduced a two-and-a-half-year sentence for a sexual assault to two years less a day. (Sentences of two years and longer are served in a federal penitentiary; shorter terms are served in a provincial jail.) The man was carrying a gun as he abducted the woman, threatened her with death and raped her; yet the judge said the attack was "not accompanied by many of the unpleasant features that normally surround such an offence."

An Ontario farmer who was convicted of sexually assaulting six boys was described by a judge in 1981 as "a man who gets caught up in the spirit of boyish horseplay." In 1983, a judge, who heard that a thirteen year old girl had been forced to fellate one man while another sodomized her, determined that there was "no evidence of permanent injury inflicted upon the complainant." In 1985, a judge said the sexual assaults a man perpetrated on his daughters could have been "an exaggerated paramedical examination." In 1988, a district court judge acquitted a man on charges of uttering threats (of rape) against three Ottawa Rough Rider cheerleaders because, he said, rape doesn't necessarily involve physical, emotional or psychological harm.

Judges are particularly likely to minimize sexual assaults against "unworthy" victims. In 1986, a judge commented that a prostitute who was raped, urinated upon, and had a plunger used on her vagina "suffered no long-lasting psychological injury."

They are equally prone to look for mitigating factors in crimes committed by "worthy" men. One such man was sentenced to two years less a day in 1983 for sexually assaulting a thirteen-year-old girl after the judge noted that he was "having marital difficulties." Another offender was given a suspended sentence in 1981 for sexually assaulting his fifteen-year-old daughter because, the judge said, "there is an indication that the mother of the victim has a drinking problem and there were a series of separations."

In Nova Scotia, a judge ruled in 1986 that the stress of being charged was sufficient punishment for a prominent businessman who was convicted of sexually assaulting a baby-sitter. Similarly, in 1985, a judge in Manitoba noted that a former teacher who was convicted of sexually assaulting a female student had attracted negative publicity and been fired. In handing down a suspended sentence, the judge also noted that the man had received "glowing" character references, including one from the pastor of his church that said, "Winnipeg needs one hundred more like him. Give him a citation for good citizenship. He has my unqualified admiration."

An Ottawa man was given a suspended sentence in 1984 for sexually assaulting eight boys because the judge said the offender would have "a hard time" in jail if his offences became known to other inmates. In 1987, a social worker convicted of sexual abuse was also given a suspended sentence with the judicial comment that "to err is human." The judge also commented that the crime was "completely out of character," not knowing that the same man had been in court twice that week on similar charges.

A twenty-two year old man in Sault Ste. Marie, Ontario, was sentenced in 1988 to a ninety-day jail term to be served on weekends after he was convicted of following a woman out of a hotel where she was celebrating her birthday, dragging her into a nearby garden, punching her in the face until she passed out, and then sexually assaulting her. The judge said the man came from "a good family" and had learned his lesson. He also commented that the assault was not premeditated and "had an element of impulsiveness, of spontaneity" to it. When the defence lawyer informed the judge that the offender coached a soccer team on Friday nights, the judge granted a two-hour extension to the time the man had to report to jail. The Crown successfully appealed the sentence; the man was given two years less a day.

Another ninety-day intermittent sentence was handed out by an Ontario judge in 1989 to a high school track star who raped a seventeen-year-old female student. The presentence report noted that he had "prosocial values."

Members of the judicial system frequently respond to sexual assault charges by blaming the victim. Although men who wear expensive suits are not told, if they are mugged, that they provoked the attack, the attire, occupation and location of sexual assault victims is often cited as a reason either to dismiss charges or to be lenient in punishment. In 1983, a judge in Edmonton cut in half an eight-year sentence for a twice-convicted rapist who sexually assaulted a handicapped woman, remarking that the victim should have expected to be raped. "When somebody grabs a citizen off the street, we take a dim view of that," said Chief Justice William McGillivray of the Alberta Court of Appeal. "But when a lady accompanies a man home at 3:00 A.M. to drink beer and smoke marijuana, one might not be too surprised if something happened under the circumstances." The complainant, who requires leg braces, testified that her assailant kicked her crutches away and punched her in the face while assaulting her.

The same year, an Ontario Supreme Court justice acquitted a man of rape because, he said, he found it "very difficult to accept" the complainant's testimony, considering that she had answered her door at 5:30 in the morning wearing "rather skimpy attire" and did not lock it after telling the accused he could not come in.

In 1988, a Manitoba Court of Appeal judge cut in half a four-year sentence for a seventy-three year old man who sexually assaulted three girls aged ten, eleven and thirteen. The girls engaged in prostitution to earn money and took advantage of the man, the judge ruled. "The kids are not victims, but perpetrators."

Complaints about such remarks are reviewed by the Canadian Judicial Council if the judge is federally appointed; otherwise, by the relevant provincial judicial council. Although any member of the public can file an objection, typically, action is taken only when the statements are publicly reported. The council's response is not normally announced.

The attitudes within the criminal justice system towards women and children are even more evident in the judiciary's response to charges of straight physical violence. In 1989, for example, a provincial court judge in Manitoba suggested, after fining a man $300 for hitting his wife during an argument, that there might be times when men should slap women: "How does a person admonish his wife if she goes out on the town with other people, to wit, guys, drinking, and comes home late when she should have been home looking after the children or cooking or whatever else she is expected to do? Sometimes a slap in the face is all that she needs and might not be such unreasonable force after all. But here there was at least a slap in the face to which he has pleaded guilty and is willing to suffer the consequences." A judge in Nova Scotia apparently agreed. He granted an absolute discharge to a fellow magistrate for slapping his wife during an argument.

A second judge in Manitoba remarked, as he sentenced a man to probation for threatening his girlfriend at gunpoint, "Somebody once said to me, 'Women—you can't live with them, you can't live without them.'" Also in Manitoba, Liberal leader Sharon Carstairs complained when a man who beat his children received a lighter sentence than a man who beat a cat. The first offender, who almost tore off his son's ear and punched his daughter in the face, was sent to jail for a month; the second, who hit his girlfriend's cat and burned its paw on a radiator, was sentenced to two months in jail.

In Quebec in 1989, a police officer was given a conditional discharge and two years' probation after he pleaded guilty to showing up at his estranged wife's home at 4:00 A.M. and violently beating her. The court was told that the woman was dragged down the stairs by her hair, had tufts of hair pulled from her head, had her forehead cut and a finger broken in three places. The man was on duty at the time of the offence.

A 1987 study conducted in Ontario for the federal solicitor-general's department found that the police lay charges in only forty-seven percent of cases in which men beat up their wives. And judges give jail terms to only twenty percent of those convicted of wife assault; among that group, one day is the most common sentence.

But, as Donna Hackett, a Crown counsel and

senior policy advisor on justice issues to the Ontario Women's Directorate, told the Law Union of Ontario in 1987, "There is nothing mysterious about judges. They are just Joe Public as far as attitudes go."

As the Newfoundland inquiry dragged on in the fall of 1989, the possibility of changing the attitudes that led to the victimization of Mount Cashel residents by their guardians and by society appeared slim. While the witnesses were testifying in St. John's, a group of male students at Queen's University in Kingston—among the brightest and most privileged members of the upcoming generation of Canadians—were having what they later said was just some old-fashioned fun. They wanted, they said, simply to lighten up the unduly serious atmosphere of their student council's anti-rape campaign. In response to the campaign's slogan, No Means No, the men hung signs in the windows of their residence that said such things as No Means More Beer, No Means Tie Her Up, No Means Kick Her in the Teeth.

Their notion of humour is not unique. According to an editorial in *The Nation*, similar-minded young men had roamed the campus of New Jersey's Princeton University two years earlier, after a Take Back the Night march, and screamed "We can rape anybody we want."

8

The Victims

CANADIANS WHO FOLLOWED the media coverage of the 1989 Mount Cashel orphanage inquiry could have little doubt about the devastating aftermath of sexual assault. One by one, former residents, some of whom were only six years old when the abuse began, described how the experiences continue to haunt them years later. They told of impaired self-esteem, difficulty coping with aggression, and suicide attempts. Some felt that their lives were irreparably damaged; others were optimistic that they could eventually overcome their pain.

"We had part of our life stolen from us," Darren Connors told the *Globe and Mail*. "Our childhood, our innocence, our sexuality was stolen from us."

Like many others, Connors said that he had tried to take his own life since leaving Mount Cashel and that he still feels lost and purposeless. "I've been shit on so much in my life, maybe it just comes naturally to me now. You know when you are licked."

John MacIsaac told the Toronto newspaper, "I feel like there's still a void in my life, like there's something missing and I don't know what it is. But I will find it."

By the time the inquiry was two months old, it had chalked up $1 million in expenses. Not one cent had been spent on counselling for the former residents who were testifying. It was typical of government responses to the victims of sexual assault and, indeed, to the treatment needs of offenders themselves. In the face of a public outcry, governments will spend untold amounts of money on royal commissions and task forces that mollify voters but merely confirm and reconfirm the problems. Little effort is devoted to solutions.

Two provincial social workers who were assigned to oversee the orphanage in the early 1970s told the inquiry that they did not have time to make regular visits to Mount Cashel. They were supervising more than 150 juveniles on probation in St. John's. Both Brendan Devine, who held the job in 1972 but quit in frustration the next year, and his predecessor, LeRoy Norberg, testified that they had written provincial authorities recommending that an experienced social worker be hired to work full-time at the orphanage. They were informed, according to a reply read to the commission, that the government had no money for a new social worker. The task of ensuring the well-being of the boys was left to the directors of the orphanage.

It is an old story. Shortly after the Newfoundland inquiries were announced in the spring of 1989, another sex abuse scandal was uncovered in a small paper-mill town on the Quebec side of the Ottawa River, twenty-five miles northeast of Hull. Two brothers had been sexually assaulted by sixteen town residents while they waited twenty-two months to be visited by a social worker. One was eighteen months old when the abuse began; the other, three years old. During that time, the elder boy had been treated in hospital thirty-three times for burns, cuts, penis infections, stomach aches, and vomiting. By the time the abuse was made public, he was living in a psychiatric hospital; doctors said he was unable to concentrate, suffered frequent nightmares, and trembled constantly. The younger child was living in a foster home.

Officials at the Outaouais Youth Protection Service, under fire for not investigating the case when the first complaint was received in April 1985, explained that they had 450 children in need of help in the region and only nine social workers on the front lines. Across the province, they said, there were 3,000 children on the waiting lists of social service agencies. The Outaouais social workers, believing the boys were suffering only from neglect, attended to what they thought were more urgent cases. When Quebec's Committee of Youth Protection was assigned to investigate the incident, it found that the case had actually been dropped from the waiting list a few months before the police investigation began.

The case attracted publicity when the offenders appeared in court, a year after they were charged. Three days later, the *Ottawa Citizen* reported: "This week, Quebec's Health and Social Services Minister, Thérèse Lavoie-Roux, agreed to look into the waiting list problem in the Outaouais after a meeting with Quebec cabinet minister Michel Gratton, who is also Gatineau's MNA." The next day, according to the newspaper, Quebec premier Robert Bourassa, who was on a two-day election swing through the Outaouais, "hinted" that his upcoming budget would allocate more money to deal with Quebec's backlog of child abuse cases.

In 1984, a four-year study commissioned by the federal government confirmed that child sexual abuse is a major social problem. The committee, headed by

Robin Badgley, a University of Toronto professor, found that one in four females and one in eight males had been sexually assaulted, and that eighty percent of these assaults had first occurred when the victims were children or youths. The report noted, "Sexual offences are committed so frequently and against so many persons that there is an evident and urgent need to afford victims greater protection than that now being provided. . . . What is required is the recognition by all Canadians that children and youths have the absolute right to be protected from these offences. To achieve this purpose, a major shift in the fundamental values of Canadians and in social policies by government must be realized. . . . If no action is taken, or if only token programs are initiated, the risk that children and youths will continue to be sexually abused will remain intolerably high." The federal government responded by setting up a family violence-prevention division within Health and Welfare Canada and by appointing Rix Rogers, a former head of the national council of YMCAs, to draft a long-term plan of action. In April 1989, as he was preparing his final report, Rogers said he was aware that the federal and provincial governments are unlikely to be able to find a lot of money to devote to the prevention of child sex abuse, but a new approach that breaks down barriers among government ministries and among professional disciplines would help. He added that both the country's treatment services and courts have been overwhelmed by the scope of the problem. "Our children's aid societies, our courts, and our crown attorneys are virtually overloaded. . . . We have a situation now that in some cases, once a charge is laid, we are waiting two years before the case gets through the criminal courts."

In incest cases that reach the courts, it is the victims who pay the price of the delays. In a 1986 study, Camille Messier, a Quebec researcher, documented the trend for child protection agencies to take children out of their homes in such cases, which leads to children being doubly victimized. "It is the father who is the problem," she points out. "He is the person responsible for the damage done . . . but that message gets lost when the child is removed from the home . . . while the father [is allowed to remain]."

Most incidents of sexual assault do not reach the courts, however. In the case of adult victims, if the crimes are disclosed at all, it is usually to volunteers in rape crisis centres or to the small number of social workers and health care professionals who concentrate on counselling victims of sexual assault. Across Canada, this dedicated cadre is being increasingly overwhelmed by the record number of adults who are coming forward to talk about their childhood abuse and about recent assaults. The crisis centres are angry and frustrated by the meagre resources they are allocated by provincial governments to deal with the problem. "The situation is an abuse of rape crisis workers," says Pauline Duffett, the coordinator of the Ontario Coalition of Rape Crisis Centres. "We have to raise money and do the work."

In February 1990, the Ontario government announced a major increase in funding for the province's twenty rape crisis centres, bringing the average grant to $58,000 a year. However, it stated it would fund no new centres for five years. Duffett says the additional money is appreciated but that it will not allow the centres to pare down their waiting lists for group counselling or to conduct routine public education classes in high schools. In other words, she says, the centres still can do no more "than just pick up the pieces." Two years ago the coalition told the government it needed $90,000 a year per centre if it was to meet the demand for its services. The shortfall means that the centres' workers will still have to spend an enormous amount of time raising additional money through letter-writing campaigns, bake sales, and raffles. They also have to train volunteers and get on with their primary job of counselling victims. In every province other than Quebec, says Duffett, the situation is much worse.

When professionals working with sexual assault victims learned in November 1989 that the federal government had loaned millions of dollars to strip clubs in Ontario and Quebec through its Federal Business Development Bank, they were enraged. "Clearly, we are in the wrong business," remarked a Toronto crisis worker bitterly.

Dealing with the legacy of sexual assault is often a tortuous and prolonged process. Even a single incident can have devastating effects. A child in Vancouver who was sexually assaulted by a serial rapist in 1986 lost all her hair. A teenager in Ontario who was sixteen when she was dragged off the street and raped told an Ontario court, "It changed my whole life. I feel like everyone's following me—that everyone else is like [the perpetrator]. If a man looks at me, I am terrified." A young woman, who was raped the same year by a man who scaled the walls of her Toronto apartment building and broke in while she was sleeping, said, "To tell you . . . the night mare, sense of loss, grief, nausea . . . panic, darkness . . . . There was no sex, only pain. I went into shock. I felt as if I was set on fire. It lasted for days. Now I go to bed. It's nightmares. I see his face at my window. My sleep and strength are robbed in the night. I can hear him. I can smell him. I wake from my sleep, and it is as if I'm raped again."

In the same way that many soldiers returning from war had flashbacks of traumatic events, such as someone being blown up, many rape victims vividly relive their assaults. Dereck O'Brien told the *Globe and Mail* that when he was describing to Newfoundland's judicial inquiry what happened to him at a foster home before he went to the orphanage, "I could actually feel the stick hit me across the fingers. I could actually feel cold." He said he had been having nightmares since the hearing began and sometimes, while driving, found himself frozen at a green light, oblivious to the cars honking behind him.

The long-term effects of sexual assault hinge on many variables, according to Pam Benson, a Kingston therapist. In the case of rape, it depends partly on the nature of the offence and on whether it was perpetrated by a stranger or an acquaintance. "For someone who is raped by a stranger, there is always the question, 'why me?' For someone who is raped by a person close to her, in the date-rape situation, for example, there is always the sense of betrayal." But even if two women are the victims of similar assaults, one can be far more traumatized than another, depending on her personality, her life experiences, and her coping skills. Similarly, some children are more resilient than others. "It is a real trap to get into cause and effect."

A history of child sexual abuse has been uncovered, though, in a disproportionately high percentage of the populations of prisons and psychiatric hospitals. Adolescent incest victims are more likely than other youths their age to become truant and promiscuous and to run away from home. Later in life, they are more prone to suffer from depression, poor self-esteem, sexual dysfunction and substance abuse. And there is evidence that an unusually large number of men who molest children were molested themselves when they were young.

Research has shown that rape victims are generally more than twice as likely to suffer nervous breakdowns as are robbery victims and five times as likely as nonvictims. They think seriously about suicide four times more often than robbery victims, and they attempt suicide six times more often.

Victims suffer from increased fear and anxiety for at

least three years after the attack, according to recent research. Studies have also demonstrated that a woman's feelings of distress during the assault have a greater influence on her subsequent levels of fear and anxiety than the actual extent of violence.

Typically, says Benson, a rape victim goes through three phases following a sexual assault. Immediately after the attack, women are either "very upset, crying and feeling tormented" or "completely cut off." Women who fall into the second category "may talk in a very dispassionate voice. 'I-was-in-my-house. A-man-broke-in. He-raped-me.' Both are normal reactions."

For anywhere from a few weeks to many months following the assault, most victims feel afraid, vulnerable, and helpless. They often suffer from fatigue and tension headaches. They may also feel guilty about wanting revenge. "It is not unusual at all for a woman to say, 'I just want to kill him,' or 'I would like to beat him,' and then, having said that, say, 'I feel really disgusted with myself for feeling so violent.' There is an ambivalence. She has the rage, and yet it is not acceptable to her."

The second phase tends to be relatively symptom-free, says Benson. "It is as though the woman has an outward adjustment to it. Her anxiety appears to have decreased. 'It happened a long time ago. I don't have to think about it anymore.' Really, it is a denial. It is often a calm phase in her life that is ended by a dramatic event or by increased feelings of anxiety and depression."

In addition to being anxious and depressed, victims in the third phase also tend to have chronic fears and phobias. They have a strong sense of vulnerability and may isolate themselves socially, feeling somehow contaminated by their experience. They often have generalized negative feelings towards men and experience decreased pleasure in sex. "They may not even recognize that their feelings are related to the assault."

The denial stage can last for decades in victims of incest, says Benson. "I see people who were raped as children dealing with it at age thirty and older."

When the victims' reports of sexual assault are disbelieved or discounted by the individuals in whom they confide, the betrayal is repeated and the shame and embarrassment reinforced. Blamed by society, the victims often begin to blame themselves. This is particularly true of young incest victims who are told by their fathers that they are sharing a secret no one else can know about. By keeping the secret, they often feel a sense of complicity once they realize what has happened to them. Their guilt can last into adulthood unless they receive appropriate counselling.

When one of Benson's patients expresses feelings of guilt about the sexual abuse she suffered as a child, the therapist reaches to the top of a bookcase in her office and takes down two or three soft-covered dolls: Daddy, Mommy, and Child, all anatomically correct. The patient uses the dolls to recreate what happened.

"I have had women talk to me about their sexual abuse and say it was only a back rub. Now, I get them to demonstrate what 'just a back rub' is. It often means that he began by tucking her in at night and giving her a back rub. His hands would then wander down her legs and between her thighs. And eventually he would climb into bed and have intercourse with her. It could be anal or vaginal. Often the kids don't know.

"I ask them what the room was like. Incest survivors have an incredible sense of the environment. They will tell you where the mirror was, where the light was, where the closet door was, where the bed was situated.

"I get them to stage it, and then I just talk them through. First he began to rub your back and then what happened? A back rub may be part of their denial. It is also part of testing whether the therapist or whoever is listening will be willing to hear what they have to say.

They think you will be shocked, that you will be disgusted, that you will think they are dirty, that you won't want to see them anymore. They internalize that sense of blame."

Benson says the dolls are particularly effective at getting an adult survivor of incest to realize that her experience was the result of an adult betraying a child. "It takes away the focus from whether there was a part of her that felt good about it or not. And it looks at the difference in power."

Even when they accept that they were not to blame for their abuse, however, many adults are afraid to divulge the incest to other members of their families. "To get the child to go along with what is happening, the abuser will say things like, 'If you tell your mother, I might go to jail.' 'Your mother has had enough grief in her life already. If you tell, you are going to kill her.' They blackmail the child. She grows up keeping the secret in order not to break up the family. The adult survivor has to work through the same issue.

"That's one side of it. The other side is, if she tells [now] and finds out that everyone knew all along. . . ."

Sometimes, says Benson, an adult victim of incest does not remember what happened to her. "Kids who were sexually abused in their own beds will often say that one of the ways they coped with it was to imagine they weren't really there, that they were sitting on the back of the bed or in a corner of the room. They disconnected themselves from their body sensations. Probably the longer, the more abusive, and the more intense the sexual assault, the more denial and suppression there is about what happened. I have seen people who have had abortions and babies as a result of incest and have totally blocked it out."

The memories may be triggered, says Benson, by the death of the perpetrator or, for example, in the case of a woman with children, when her daughter reaches

the age at which she was abused. They may read
something or see something on television that suddenly
brings it all back, although "part of the denial is that
they don't go to see the film *The Accused*. They don't
turn on the documentary on TV about incest. . . . When
people tell me they saw something that made them
realize [their trauma], it was usually an accident." Sometimes victims are haunted by irrational fears without
being aware of their source. "A woman may go crazy
when her husband grows a mustache, for example, or
when he gets a job where he has to wear a uniform."

Often, victims of incest will seek therapy when
they become involved in a loving relationship in which
they want to be able to trust their partner. Still, they
may be unaware of the cause of their problems.
"Frequently, the presentation I get is from a family
doctor for a woman who has sexual problems, who is
nonorgasmic. I always ask four or five pointed questions
about family violence, incest, sexual abuse as a child,
and rape. If she comes in for headaches, I ask."

Only recently have therapists started to recognize
what they now call the "disguised presentation" of an
incest survivor. Although the theory is not universally
accepted by health care professionals, Benson's experiences have convinced her that some patients have no
conscious memories of their childhood sexual abuse. In
other cases, women will deny the abuse unless they are
asked the right question.

"I had one woman I knew had been sexually
abused; you get a sort of second sense about this sort of
thing after you have been working in it for a while. I
knew it in my heart. But, 'No, no, no.' Do you remember? 'No, no, no.' Did your father ever . . . ? 'No, no,
no.' I saw her for a year and she disappeared for a year.
Then she came back and sat down in my office and
looked at me and said, 'It was my brother.' I said,
'What?' She said, 'It wasn't my father; it was my broth-

er.' I said, 'Why didn't you tell me it was your brother?'
She said, 'Because you didn't ask me.'"

Bette Solomon, another Kingston therapist who
works primarily with sexual assault victims, agrees it
often takes people some time to acknowledge what has
happened. "I've seen women who have been in and out
of psychiatric units, had every diagnosis in the book,
and never discussed sexual abuse. They have been seen
as personality disorders, hysterical women, or just
difficult. . . . When I ask them about it, they often
vehemently deny the possibility. . . . They can go from
being adamant that they were never sexually abused to
knowing that they were, but not remembering anything, to remembering the easy stuff first and then the
difficult stuff. People allow themselves to remember
what they can bear."

Solomon says women who were sexually abused as
children are encouraged by society's attitudes not to
deal with the issue. "They are given a strong message
that 'there is no use dwelling on this. Just shape up and
get on with it.' And they do." However, just because a
woman appears to have overcome a history of sexual
assault does not mean she is not still suffering. "People
talk about 'high-functioning' survivors as though they
are higher in the hierarchy or something. Women who
are very successful in their careers, for example. As
long as they can keep proving they are okay, they can
keep going. Their defence system is so good that they
might never open up. But that doesn't mean they don't
continue with the pain. And they are never going to get
over it until they face it. I am beginning to think that
people who are so-called more messed up are much
better off. They deal with it earlier."

While adults may deny the abuse they suffered as
children, Solomon says, they often hang on to the
coping skills that they used to get through the experience—
behaviours that as adults interfere with their relation-

ships with other people. "At the time, it may have been really adaptive to learn to manipulate or to lie to people in order to save their necks or to deny their own feelings. But those coping skills end up being symptoms because they are no longer protecting them. They are just getting in the way of them living life. If they are not in touch with what they are feeling, for example, they might behave very angrily when they are hurt and alienate everyone."

It is not uncommon, says Solomon, for a victim of incest to admit that her father sexually abused her and then retract it: "They have so much terror and ambivalence about betraying the offending parent. . . . The more pathological the relationship between a parent and a child, the more tied to that parent they are. They might stay at home until they are adults. In order for children to move away from parents, they have to have self-esteem and a personality of their own. If a child has had a happy, healthy relationship with the parent, it is much easier to leave the nest. If you have been abused, you are much more likely to be tied in a very sick way to those parents. There is always the need for approval to wipe out the badness—approval that never comes."

When an incest survivor begins to deal with her abuse in therapy, she will initially feel worse than she did when she was denying it. She may have nightmares, or flashbacks of the assaults. The pain must be endured if she is to recover. First, she must empathize with herself as a child. "Once that happens," says Solomon, "individuals go through a whole mourning process. They are angry and then really sad about all the losses. Not just the loss of their childhood but the loss of relationships, the loss of self love. . . ." Without opening up the wounds and working through the process, though, "it is hard to move on. You keep giving the rest of your life to the perpetrator. In a way, you are revictimizing yourself."

When women understand how their experience has affected their lives, says Benson, they can begin to change the way they respond to things. More important, they can stop working so hard to try to forget what happened. "When they bring it up to consciousness and work through it, they don't have to spend that energy anymore pushing it away. They talk in terms of feeling free. They say they can get on with their life."

It is not easy working with sexual assault victims, says Benson: "When you do this kind of work, it brings into bold relief all of your own fears about being violated. You not only have to help the client, but you have to help yourself at the same time. I've had days when I saw five or six clients and I went home totally paranoid. Never mind checking the back seat of my car. I've checked every closet in my house. Psychologically, doing that work all day has made me feel unsafe. It is very difficult sometimes trying to comprehend that people can do this to one another. I can see only about fifteen cases at a time and only five or six really intensive cases. I have to maintain my sanity."

One of the ways she does so is to participate in informal gatherings of a group of women doing similar work. "It is really important for professionals in this field to have support, good relationships with other people, and opportunities for education. In the absence of those three things, I think you would burn out very quickly."

There are days, says Benson, "when I think what I would really like to do is to be a checkout clerk at Zellers." But that is only a fleeting fantasy. "It is really important to me that I do this work. I don't believe I have any choice. Morally, I have to do it."

If it was not for such devotion on the part of the professionals and volunteers working with the victims of sexual crimes, many rape crisis centres and other private support services for women and children would not have survived. We should not assume, however, that they can maintain their commitment indefinitely in the face of unreliable and inadequate provincial government funding that forces them to operate on shoestring budgets under the constant threat of having to shut down. Nor can the paid frontline workers like those at provincially funded children's protective agencies be expected to struggle indefinitely with unreasonable case-loads created by staff shortages. In the absence of a strong indication that society considers their work to be important and is prepared to support it adequately, the individuals dealing with victims in all arenas could eventually react to their job pressures by quitting or becoming jaded or indifferent.

If we are to confront the widespread problem of sexual crimes, we have to do more than just support the victims and treat the offenders, though. We must eradicate the attitudes that condone and even encourage sexual assault in the first place. We can start by changing the negative views of women and children perpetuated by the media, especially through pornography.

9

The Link to Pornography

ON THE EVE of his execution in January 1989, when all hope of a reprieve was gone, Ted Bundy appeared before television cameras for the last time. In an occasionally tearful interview inside Florida State Prison, America's notorious serial killer recounted how his progressive use of pornography eventually led him to act out his fantasies and sexually mutilate and murder at least thirty women. Bundy told James Dobson, a California psychologist and broadcaster, that his appetite for increasingly violent and graphic pornography was whetted at about the age of twelve when he first encountered the type of "soft" pornography commonly sold in corner grocery stores. "Like an addiction, you keep craving something which is harder, harder, something which gives you a greater sense of excitement, until you reach the point where the pornography only goes so far. You reach that jumping-off point where you're beginning to wonder if maybe actually doing it would give you that which is beyond just reading about it or looking at it."

Dorothy Lewis, a psychiatrist hired by Bundy's lawyers, later revealed to reporters that the killer was first exposed to pornography as a preschooler when he used to sneak into his family's greenhouse to look at a collection hidden by his grandfather, a man she described as "extremely violent and frightening."

While reiterating that he accepted full responsibility for his crimes, Bundy told Dobson that he believed his repeated exposure to violence, particularly sexual violence, in various media fuelled his perverse dreams and eroded his inhibitions against acting them out. Six years earlier, Bundy had talked to journalists about a "malignant entity" within him who would purchase pornography and then become excited by imagining that he was the one inflicting pain and humiliation on women while possessing them as objects. Just as his pornography consumption followed a progressive course, he said, his murderous spree began with window peeping and stalking women.

Although Bundy appeared to have nothing to gain by identifying pornography as one of the major causes of his sex crimes, some observers have commented that the killer, contrary to what he claimed, was merely trying to distance himself from his heinous deeds. But evidence of the use of pornography by other sex offenders, combined with the latest research findings by social scientists, suggests otherwise.

Canada's worst serial killer, Clifford Olson, carried a briefcase full of pornography as he drove around British Columbia in rental cars hunting down the eleven children that he savagely murdered over a nine-month period in 1980–1981. It was two years earlier that the police in Sydney, Nova Scotia, had found pornographic pictures of young children in Olson's luggage, which they recovered from his hotel room after he escaped during questioning about an indecent assault on a seven year old girl. Most of the photographs were Polaroid snapshots of the girl posing in the nude.

Fernand Robinson told the jury at his murder trial in 1984 that he had flipped through the pages of rape and bondage magazines as he fondled a young Toronto lawyer in the basement of her apartment building immediately before stabbing her repeatedly and slashing her throat. He was fifteen years old at the time.

When James Patrick Jones, a former television cameraman, was arrested in 1987 in Kamloops, British Columbia, for sexually assaulting and brutally beating to death the three year old daughter of close friends, police searching his home found a locked case containing a selection of sex toys and pornographic materials dealing with bondage. The young girl's uncle was shocked that his friend of eight years, a man he described as kind, generous, and thoughtful, was capable of such an atrocity. "He was a good friend to us. I just can't believe it."

Pornography collections were also discovered in the home of David Dobson, an eighteen year old Toronto factory worker, who sexually attacked and sadistically beat to death a female hitchhiker in 1982, and in the apartment of Kenneth Steingard, the Manitoba rapist who killed four people in 1985 before turning a gun on himself.

Obviously, all viewers of pornography do not go on to brutalize women and children, but there is mounting evidence that in susceptible men, the material feeds and legitimizes their deviant sexual tendencies. Gene Abel, director of the Sexual Behaviour Clinic at the New York Psychiatric Institute, told the United States Attorney General's Commission on Pornography in 1985 that his research indicated that more than fifty percent of sex offenders use pornography. Furthermore, Abel testified, the rapists and child molesters who do use pornography are less able to control their deviant behaviours than are offenders who do not. The link between pornography and sex offences was given further support by the results of a study conducted at the Kingston Sexual Behaviour Clinic, also presented to the commission. In a survey of eighty-nine sex offenders who attended the clinic over a six-year period, one-third reported that they had used pornography immediately prior to at least one of their crimes. Although these men were all outpatients, they nevertheless included some rapists and child molesters who had injured their victims in a sadistic manner.

As the quantity and scope of pornography have grown over the past decade, so, too, has the evidence from social scientists that such material has a negative influence on many who view it. In reviewing these findings, we will separate sexual stimuli into various categories. (We acknowledge that not everyone will agree with our definitions; they are intended merely to clarify the data that follow.)

While both erotica and pornography are designed to arouse the viewer, we will use the term erotica to refer to portrayals of adult men and women engaging in affectionate, consenting sexual relations in which both partners are apparently in positions of equal power. Conversely, the generic label pornography will pertain to explicit or implicit depictions of sexual activity in which there is an apparent power imbalance or where one of the partners is not consenting, is being degraded or humiliated, or is seen only as a sex object.

The term "soft-core" pornography is applied to materials that do not explicitly depict sexual acts, although such acts may be simulated or implied. "Hard-core" pornography refers to graphic displays of sexual activity. These graphic displays are often violent, involving the use of force by one or more persons against another or others in the enactment of sex.

Although soft-core pornography is not graphic or violent, it is often degrading, depicting scenes in which a person (almost always a woman) is consenting but in a clearly submissive role, apparently sexually insatiable and usually subjected to some form of humiliating behaviour.

All pornography portrays sex in an impersonal or dehumanizing manner, depicting women purely as objects in a nonaffectionate context. Typically, women are portrayed as desiring repeated sex of almost any kind with almost any partner, sometimes including animals. Even when women are raped, violent pornography suggests, they usually become aroused to orgasm regardless of how brutal or degrading the attack. This reinforces the myth that all women secretly want a man to be forceful and only keep their desires hidden to avoid social disapproval. In these scenarios, rarely is a man punished in any way, regardless of his behaviour.

The production of pornography has burgeoned into a $10-billion industry in North America. But pornography is, after all, only an exaggerated and blatant expression of the antifemale and antichild sentiments that pervade the media, particularly advertising. Half-naked women lounge over the latest-model cars, hang on the arms of men who drink a particular beer, lie at the feet of men who use a certain after-shave, and chase down the street after men wearing a popular brand of jeans. Some advertisements are even more obviously degrading of women. A recent magazine promotion for Georges Marciano's Guess? jeans showed a dishevelled young blonde woman lying in a cattle pen with a man opening her shirt to reveal her breasts. An advertisement for the television series *Dynasty* pictured three of the show's lead actresses under the heading Bitch, Bitch, Bitch.

Children are also used by advertisers to appeal to

men. An advertisement for a popular perfume features a young girl of about six years of age lying on her side staring directly into the camera in a sultry fashion. She is heavily made up and is wearing a wig. The caption reads, "You see, Innocence is sexy after all." Several years ago, a soft drink manufacturer was forced to cancel a commercial on Canadian television after a particularly observant viewer complained that the teenage girl featured in the film clip was not wearing any underwear. The actress finished a song and dance sequence by somersaulting towards the camera. To the average person, it appeared innocent. But when the scene was scanned in slow motion by police, her exposed vagina was clearly visible.

The sexual images pervasive in much advertising convey essentially the same message as pornography: women and children are the servants of men's desires, and for the most part, they wish to be. When movies, television shows, and other popular media offer similar sentiments about men's power and the inferior status of women and children, they increase the likelihood that the myths of pornography will be accepted as truths.

Unfortunately Canada's laws governing pornography focus more on genitalia than on portrayals of inequality. All depictions of explicit sexual behaviour are prohibited in this country, even if both partners are clearly consenting and display affection for one another. However, the law permits implicit portrayals of dehumanizing sex. In other words, any genital or oral-genital contact is illegal, regardless of the context. But it is legal to portray a woman in a servile position with her open mouth an inch from a towering man's erect penis. Scenes of implicit sex that include violence are banned, but the aggression must be overt. A single photograph of a man's hand raised over a woman's bare buttocks, for example, would not be considered violent, even if there were red marks on her skin. Finally, depictions of sexual acts involving children, animals, or perverse fetishes are also against the law. Curiously, though, while it is against the law to produce, distribute, sell, or mail any obscene material, it is not illegal to buy, possess, or view it. And pornographers and consumers alike exploit this loophole.

Mail-order houses, many of them in California, openly advertise illegal materials in so-called soft-porn magazines commonly sold in Canada. A recent advertisement in *Swank* magazine for Down 'N Dirty Videos includes a photograph of a girl who looks about ten years old obviously fellating a man, although there is a black circle covering his penis and her mouth. In the unlikely event that the girl's apparent young age goes unnoticed by a potential buyer, the titles—"Tender and Tight," "Innocent Darlings," "Neighbour's Daughter," and "Tiny Titties," among others—spell out what the producer is offering in these ninety-minute movies, complete with sound tracks. Another advertisement in the same issue contains a photograph of a man about to have vaginal intercourse with a young girl who appears to be wearing a training bra. This film is entitled "Beginner's Luck." A third advertisement, purporting to have been placed by a married woman, hawks pictures and videos of "home sex with my husband and two girls." The list goes on.

As hard-core pornography consumers know, it is rarely necessary to write away for such illegal materials; much of it is available under the counter and, in the case of nonviolent explicit sex, often right on the shelves for customers of the thousands of neighbourhood variety stores and video outlets across the country that also sell soft-core pornography. In Metropolitan Toronto, the only city in Canada with a full-time pornography and hate-literature squad, eight police officers spend much of their time following up complaints about corner stores whose displays of cellophane-wrapped "men's magazines" include issues featuring explicit sex. Informed buyers know from the price what to expect. Legal soft-porn publications such as *Penthouse* and *Playboy* sell for $5 or $6; illegal magazines usually cost between $12 and $25. Recently, the squad also laid charges against a large Yonge Street newsvendor after a store employee allegedly popped open a secret drawer at the front counter and showed an undercover officer a generous selection of illegal videotapes selling for about $100 apiece.

With a little effort, consumers can tap into the underground networks offering illegal materials that cater to specific fetishes: sadomasochistic situations; scenes of pregnant and lactating women having sex with men or other women; people having sex with animals or urinating and defecating on one another. All of this material links deviant behaviours with pleasurable sexual sensation. In one videotape confiscated by Toronto's pornography squad, a naked woman bends over a chair as a man ties her in place and shouts obscenities at her. Once she is immobilized, he gives her an obviously painful enema and then has equally painful anal intercourse with her, while slapping her hard on the buttocks. In another film seized by the squad, an adult man rubs his penis up and down the vagina of a naked four year old girl as her older sister holds her down. The terrified look on the victim's face, as she looks around desperately for help, is an image most viewers could not forget.

Pornography became big business in North America in the 1980s when technological advances such as videocassette recorders, personal computers, pay television and specialized telephone services became part of everyday life. Today, consumers who are tired of merely scanning images and want to participate in "unusual" verbal sexual activities can call legal dial-a-porn operations and indulge their most bizarre fantasies by talking to real, live women with nicknames like Bitch Goddess. If they prefer, they can pay simply to eavesdrop. Either way, they can charge their entertainment to their VISA, American Express or MasterCard accounts. In its first year of operation in 1983, one dial-a-porn service in the United States received 180 million calls. Similarly, pornographic software companies offer computer users the opportunity to be part of the action. Incorporating high-quality graphics and animation capabilities, the programs allow players not only to move figures around on the screen, but to undress them, shackle, gag, handcuff, and rape them. To enhance the you-are-there feeling, the software, dubbed with such titles as The Carnal Knowledge Navigator, has been programmed to emit appropriate sounds. The more expensive personalized versions include the user's name.

Pornography is meant to be entertaining. Whether intended or not, it is also informative. It is inconsistent to claim that advertising produces attitudinal and behavioural shifts in viewers while insisting that pornography has no such effect. In 1985, shortly after the federal government prohibited tobacco companies from sponsoring sporting events, the Canadian Coalition Against Media Pornography made this point in a brief to a parliamentary subcommittee on equality rights: "It is clear there is a widely held belief that behaviour is modelled. If a picture of an athlete smoking is assumed to promote the belief that smoking is healthy and acceptable, then why is it so difficult to accept that a picture of a man holding a power drill to a woman's vagina will promote the belief that such behaviour is acceptable in our society?"

Early theorists believed that men would either become bored by repeated use of pornography or, in the case of individuals with deviant interests, would use it as a safety valve to satisfy their desires. Neither of these views has been found to be true. Numerous studies over the past decade have documented the negative influences of violent pornography on the attitudes of viewers. Even if they do not actually reenact the violent scenes witnessed, men who view material that depicts women enjoying rape and other forms of sexual violence are more accepting of violence against women and of rape myths; they have more rape fantasies, and they report a greater willingness to commit rape themselves.

After viewing scenes of rape, the proportion of men who admit at least some likelihood that they would commit a sexual assault if they were sure not to be caught is rarely less than thirty-five percent and has been as high as sixty-five percent. Furthermore, the increased tendency occurs irrespective of social class, intellect, or educational attainment.

Neil Malamuth, a psychologist now working in the United States who did much of his early work at the University of Manitoba, has repeatedly found that even brief exposures to violent pornography can lead to a more callous attitude towards rape and women in general. In studies on the effects of pornography, participants are carefully counselled before being dismissed from the laboratory. (The researchers thoroughly explain that the depictions the men have seen do not truthfully describe the real desires of women, and that, in fact, women are repulsed by forced sex. Evidence is also presented on the harmful effects of sexual assault on victims. Finally, the subjects are told that the sexual elements in the film are so explicit that some degree of arousal by them is to be expected and does not indicate propensity to rape a woman. This debriefing procedure has been proven to eliminate any negative attitudes the participants may have acquired during the study.) The average pornography consumer, however, is not debriefed and in some cases exposure to scenes of forced sex initiates a process that eventually culminates in an overt sexual attack.

A fifteen year old boy who was referred to the Kingston clinic after being incarcerated for raping a girl two years his senior said he was simply duplicating what he had seen in one of several X-rated videotapes he watched at a friend's home. The movie, which belonged to his companion's father, showed a woman being forced at knifepoint to participate in fellatio and anal and vaginal intercourse. The young offender was average-looking and had a pleasant personality, but he was shy around girls and afraid to initiate conversations with them. The more he watched the tape, the more excited he became. He could fulfil his dream of having sex with a girl, he realized, even though he was socially unskilled, simply by using force. After several months of surreptitious screenings, he set out one night with a piece of rope and a knife in search of a victim. When he found one, he dragged her into a park, tied her up, and did exactly what he had seen the film's rapist do.

Similarly, a thirty-three year old Brampton, Ontario, security guard told a county court judge that he was merely acting out what he had seen in an illegal porn video when he sexually molested four girls, aged seven to nine. Although he described himself as a "filthy animal," he also testified that he did not use force on his victims—"they wanted to do it."

There are two ways such men can be affected by the pornographic scenarios they have seen. The first is desensitization. Desensitization is part of the human experience; it happens with pornography just as it happens with any other emotionally provocative presentation. Many of us who watched television footage of the Vietnam war from the comfort of our living rooms twenty years ago were profoundly horrified by what we saw. Now we watch films containing much more gruesome scenes and call it entertainment. In the same way, repeated exposure to violent depictions of rape will cause some viewers to disregard the negative impact on the victims and focus instead on the assailants' apparent pleasure and freedom from punishment.

The second way pornography can affect the viewer is by provoking imitation, which again is a common experience. Indeed, the eminent psychologist Albert Bandura claims that this is the primary basis for all human learning. When we see activities that lead consistently to desirable outcomes—in this case, sexual gratification—with no negative consequences, the probability of at least some of us imitating them is very high. Repeated sexual arousal to these scenes can eventually break down the viewer's inhibitions and cause him to attack a victim.

Few people would be surprised to learn that violent pornography has harmful effects; surveys have shown that sixty percent of Canadians support the current ban on depictions of forced sex. Until recently, however, there was a common belief that nonviolent but degrading pornography—the type commonly featured in soft-porn magazines—had little or no antisocial effect. New studies refute that view. In fact, they show that depictions of noncoercive but degrading sex might even be more harmful than violent pornography.

In a 1987 ground-breaking study of 426 "normal" men, James Check, a professor of psychology at York University in Toronto, examined the effects of three sets of videotapes portraying intercourse between a man and a woman. In the first set of tapes, the woman was raped and portrayed as enjoying the experience. In the second, there was no overt violence or coercion, but the woman was treated as an object with no human qualities other than her physical attributes, and she was verbally abused, dominated, and degraded; again, she was represented as liking the experience. The third set of tapes consisted of scenes of erotica—mutually consenting, affectionate sexual interactions with neither violence nor dehumanizing content. The participants in the study were divided into four groups: the first three each watched a different set of the sex videos; the fourth group (the controls) viewed nonsexual scenes.

Roughly a quarter of the men were university students; the others had been recruited through newspaper advertisements. Their occupations ranged from truck drivers to doctors, and their ages from eighteen to seventy-eight with a mean age of thirty-two. Half were single, and two-thirds had post-secondary school education of some kind. After watching the videotapes over six days, all the men were asked how likely they were to rape a woman if they were sure they would not be caught or punished. The results showed that the tapes of noncoercive but degrading sex had exactly the same effect on the men's attitudes as tapes of rape. Twenty percent of those who saw either the violent sex *or* the degrading sex reported at least some likelihood that they would commit rape, compared to only ten percent of the control group. Furthermore, when they were asked to rate their propensity to force a woman to perform unwanted sexual acts, the men who viewed the noncoercive degrading videos indicated they were slightly more likely to do so than those who saw the violent tapes—thirty-nine percent compared to thirty-four percent. The effect of erotica on the subjects, however, was found to be insignificant.

Check has also found that nonoffending men with a stated propensity to rape have the same sort of negative and hostile attitudes towards women commonly expressed by rapists. He has demonstrated, too, that they tend to be solitary men who lack empathy and disregard danger.

Other studies, including one conducted at the Kingston Sexual Behaviour Clinic, have confirmed Check's findings. In the Kingston study, undertaken in 1986 by Bonnie Seidman, eighty nonoffending males were exposed to one of five different "preparatory" videotapes, followed for all subjects by a rape tape and a consenting-sex tape. One of the preliminary videos portrayed the countryside and was devoid of sexual content; two illustrated consenting sexual behaviour, one implicit and one explicit; two more were implicit and explicit depictions of forced sex. The implicit tapes involved simulated intercourse between naked partners, focusing primarily on the couples' interactions, although it was clear that penetration had been achieved. The explicit tapes concentrated on the genitals of the man and woman.

Men who viewed the countryside scene first subsequently showed greater sexual arousal to portrayals of consenting sex than they did to rape. Subjects who saw either the implicit or explicit rape tapes were later equally aroused to both consenting and forced sex; so were the males who saw the explicit version of the consenting sex scene which, because it focused on genital interactions and was devoid of any affectionate component, was more like degrading pornography than erotica even though it did not include clearly humiliating acts. The men who initially saw the tape of affectionate, consenting simulated sex were later more aroused by tapes of consenting sex than were the men who saw the nature scene first. This finding seems to suggest that viewing affectionate, consenting sex, or erotica, could have beneficial effects and might be useful in sex education.

The fact that depictions of impersonal sex in which women are degraded or dehumanized leads to callous sexual attitudes in some viewers, even when these depictions contain no violence, tends to substantiate what feminists have been arguing for years. It is the imbalance of power portrayed between men and women in pornography that is the essence of its pernicious nature. Whether these power imbalances are conveyed by force on the part of the man, degrading behaviours on the part of either participant, or personal indifference on the part of the male and submissiveness by the female may not be as important as some theorists would like to believe.

Albert Bandura's studies on aggression reinforce this perspective. Bandura has investigated ways of overcoming the usual constraints that prevent people from acting aggressively towards one another. He and his colleagues have found that the more they make the victims appear different from the aggressors, the easier it is for the aggressors to be cruel to the subjects. This is just what pornography does. It exaggerates the differences between men and women and makes women seem like nonhuman objects.

In the early 1980s, Dolf Zillmann and Jennings Bryant, two American communications researchers, examined the effects on nonoffending males of six weeks of repeated viewing of degrading but noncoercive sex videos. They found that many of the viewers wished to emulate certain behaviours they had seen as well as some unconventional sexual acts that were not depicted in the tapes—acts that they had described prior to the study as being offensive and undesirable. The men had also changed their opinions about the prevalence of behaviours such as anal intercourse and bestiality, believing them to be much more common than they had held originally. After viewing the videos, the men thought that promiscuity was more widespread and acceptable than they had reported previously, and they were less satisfied with and trusting of their own sexual partners.

It is not only men who are negatively affected by depictions of impersonal sex. Several researchers have documented that women who are exposed to materials that portray females as sex objects and as nondiscriminating in their partners are just as likely as male viewers to trivialize rape, to view a rape victim as promiscuous, and to be more lenient than a control group in meting out punishment to a rapist in a mock trial.

Adults are not the only viewers of pornography, however. In considering who might be vulnerable to its insidious influences, we must not forget children. Check has shown that the highest users of explicit pornography are males between the ages of twelve and seventeen. A survey Bryant conducted of six hundred students and adults in the United States showed that one hundred percent of boys in high school and ninety-two percent of boys in junior high school had read *Playboy* magazine. The first time they viewed these magazines they were, on average, eleven years old. The older students had seen an average of sixteen issues; the younger students, an average of five. Bryant found that the average age at which junior high school boys had watched a hard-core, X-rated sexually explicit film was fourteen years, eight months; ninety-two percent said they had seen at least one. Bryant's study also indicated that younger viewers have a greater desire to imitate what they have seen in X-rated pornography than do older viewers. Other studies have confirmed that early exposure to pornography makes it more likely that viewers will commit sex offences as adults.

Since all men are not adversely affected by exposure to pornography, it would be beneficial to understand who is at greatest risk. Most researchers consider that the life experiences of men influence their susceptibility to the messages of pornography.

Many male children who do not develop confidence when they are young are ill-prepared to interact in a socially positive manner with female peers in adolescence and young adulthood. These young males tend to follow paths that will artificially bolster their self-image and make them feel powerful and in control. Material depicting males in control, either through the use of force or threats or by virtue of a woman's or a child's submission, can have special appeal to these males. In addition, males who are socially unskilled and who lack self-confidence may find such pornography attractive because it clearly suggests that females are eager to please any male. Sexual satisfaction, such materials say, can be had without the taxing efforts of establishing a relationship. Similarly, males who were raised in families in which violence by the father against the mother and children was commonplace can be expected to model their father's successful strategy and use forcefulness in the pursuit of their own needs— sexual or other. This type of developmental history is typical of sex offenders. Accordingly, we would expect these men to be among the most vulnerable to the effects of pornography.

There have not been any controlled studies with sex offenders in which they have been exposed to pornography and then had their attitudes, sexual responsiveness, or levels of aggression assessed. Researchers who have attempted to examine the more direct connection between pornography and sexual assault have either looked at the relationship between the availability of legal pornography and the corresponding rates of sexual offences or at the offenders' current responses to pornography or their reported use of it.

Examining the relationship between the availability of pornography and the rates of sex offending is fraught with difficulties. It is quite possible that the same antiwomen sentiments that encourage the widespread dissemination of pornography also create a climate in which sex offending is inevitably high. And relying on an offender's reports of his pornography use poses as many problems in terms of proving whether pornography played a role in his offences as does measuring his current arousal to deviant sexual acts. However, there are no examples of regions with widespread pornography and low rates of sexual crimes, and there are no studies showing that the majority of sex offenders either have not used or do not respond to pornography. The absence of any confirming data certainly weakens the claim that pornography has no direct harmful effects.

One of the most widely cited studies on the relationship between the availability of pornography and the rate of sexual assault was conducted in Denmark during the 1960s. The results of this investigation were reported by Beryl Kutchinsky, a Danish social scientist who pointed out that the number of sex crimes had decreased since the country's liberalizing of laws against pornography. However, some sex offences, such as prostitution and pornography distribution, were listed as sex crimes prior to the early 1960s but not thereafter. The main offence that did show a decrease was exhibitionism, and Kutchinsky later showed that this reduction was due to the fact that women no longer bothered to report these crimes. When data on the frequency of rape was examined by other researchers, as well as by the Copenhagen police, it was clear that violent sexual assaults had increased rather than decreased.

John Court, an Australian psychologist, found that as the constraints on the availability of pornography were lifted in Denmark, Sweden, Great Britain, the United States, New Zealand, and Australia, the rates of rape in those countries increased. In perhaps his most compelling example, Court analyzed the incidence of rape in two Australian states between 1964 and 1977, when South Australia liberalized its laws on pornography and Queensland maintained its conservative policy. Over the thirteen-year period, the number of rapes in Queensland remained at the same low level—3 to 4 per 100,000 at risk—while South Australia's rate, which was lower than Queensland's in 1964, showed a sixfold increase. Similar data from New Zealand show that the incidence of rape increased from 4 per 100,000 at risk before the 1964 liberalization of the laws on obscenity to a peak of 9 per 100,000 before the 1974 reintroduction of restrictions. By 1978, the rate had decreased to 7 per 100,000.

Recent research in the United States has strengthened Court's claim of a connection between widespread pornography consumption and high sexual assault rates. In these American studies conducted in the mid-1980s, sociologists at the University of New Hampshire compared the circulation of eight soft-core porn magazines with the crime rate in each state. Not only did the data reveal a high correlation between the proliferation of these magazines and the incidence of rape, it showed a low correlation between the sales of these magazines and other violent crimes, including murder and aggravated assault.

Gene Abel was the first researcher to describe the different responses to pornography by various categories of sex offenders. Rapists, according to his studies, are equally aroused by audio and videotape depictions of consenting and forced sex, while other sex offenders show greater arousal to consenting sex. Similar research at the Clarke Institute of Psychiatry indicated that the sadistic rapists (those who have a history of exceptional violence and cruelty in their offences and have typically attacked many more women than have other rapists) show the greatest preference for portrayals of forced sex. Related research with child molesters has shown that the most dangerous of these men have the highest response to scenes of sex with children.

While early reports indicated that sex offenders had no greater experience with pornography than other men, the reliability of these studies is questionable. Many of the investigations were conducted inside jails, where the offenders' distrust of professionals is usually the strongest. The data were frequently collected in one interview by a researcher previously unknown to the inmates, and the men in the control group were often quite different from the offenders in ways that almost guaranteed that their use of pornography would be greater. (For example, in one study, the control subjects were chosen from men who admitted to being high users of pornography.)

The findings of one of these projects were accepted both by the United States Commission on Obscenity and Pornography, which met in the late 1960s, and by the more recent Attorney General's Commission on Pornography as evidence that sex offenders make little use of pornography. Michael Goldstein, a psychologist, compared the reported use of twenty categories of pornography among rapists and child molesters and various nonoffending males, including heterosexuals, homosexuals, and transvestites. None of these categories described sex with children, only two described forced sex, and only one described homosexuality. Since the index of pornography use was the number of categories checked, it is no wonder that the heterosexual nonoffenders seemed to have greater exposure to pornography. If all the categories had been child pornography, the child molesters may well have been shown to have the greatest exposure and the heterosexual little or none.

Although its methodology renders it generally unsatisfactory, the Goldstein study does reveal eccentricities among some sex offenders in their responses to pornography. Eighty percent of the rapists who were exposed to various types of pornography as teenagers said they wished to emulate the acts they saw depicted, whereas only forty-eight percent of nonoffenders who were exposed to similar material said they wished to imitate it. Asked whether they would like to own pornography, forty-six percent of the rapists, fifty percent of the heterosexual pedophiles, and fifty-nine percent of the homosexual pedophiles said yes, compared with twenty-nine percent of the nonoffending men. All of the rapists who expressed this desire actually had pornography collections, as did eighty-three percent of the heterosexual pedophiles and eighty percent of the homosexual pedophiles. Among the nonoffending group, only half of those who expressed an interest in owning pornography—fifteen percent of the total group—did own it.

In the same study, thirty percent of the rapists claimed to have been exposed to pornography between the ages of six and ten, compared with only two percent of the nonoffending group. Other research has shown that exposure to pornography prior to the age of fourteen is linked to greater involvement as an adult in deviant sexual practices, particularly rape.

In the six-year survey conducted at the Kingston Sexual Behaviour Clinic, offenders and matched non-offending males were asked about their exposure to, and use of, three types of pornography: nonconsenting violent sex (i.e. rape); sex involving children; and consenting sexual relations between a man and a woman. Unfortunately, at that time, the researchers were not aware of the importance of distinguishing degrading consenting sex from affectionate depictions, so the latter category included both.

Approximately one-third of the rapists and nonfamilial child molesters reported being exposed to at least one form of sexually explicit pornography during puberty, while none of the incest offenders had. Asked about their current habits, eighty-three percent of the rapists, sixty-seven percent of the nonfamilial pedophiles and fifty-three percent of the incest offenders reported at least occasional use of these materials, compared to only twenty-nine percent of the nonoffenders.

Most of the subjects, including the control group, claimed that at pubescence, their exposure to pornography was limited to stimuli depicting consenting but impersonal sex; as adults, the offenders, with the exception of the incest offenders, shifted to more deviant forms of pornography.

One quite unexpected finding from the Kingston study was the admission by half of the rapists that they had used impersonal but consenting sexual stimuli to fantasize about raping a woman. This reinforces the argument that such materials are as harmful as violent pornography because they present women as objects rather than as human beings with feelings as valid as men's.

The antisocial effects of impersonal pornography are clearly illustrated by the case of a married man in his early twenties who was referred to the Kingston clinic by the police after he had made sexual advances towards a twelve year old girl who had been babysitting his daughter. The adolescent had been in Claude's home twice a week for more than a year when he tried to molest her. She told the police he had been pleasant and respectful to her up until that time, except that in the previous six weeks, he had been unusually friendly and somewhat odd in her presence.

Claude had had no earlier troubles with the law and loved his wife and child. He claimed not to have had any former thoughts of deviant sex and never previously to have sought out pornography. Claude's background did not reveal any of the features typical of most sex offenders. He came from a good home where he had received affection from his parents, and he remains in a good, affectionate relationship with his family. In other words, Claude did not seem like the sort of person who would be vulnerable to the negative influence of pornography.

Over the course of several interviews with a psychologist, Claude traced his use of pornography over the previous two years. He had wanted to spice up his sex life, he said, and although he was handsome, articulate, and had a number of women friends, he did not consider engaging in an extramarital affair. Instead, he decided to reverse the declining sexual satisfaction he was feeling in his four-year-old marriage through sex aids and magazines featuring consenting adult sex, purchased at a local store.

The magazines did not seem to help, so Claude returned to the store and bought a videotape with similar content. His sexual relations with his wife reached new highs for a while but then, even with fresh videotapes, they fell off. When Claude explained his frustration to the owner of the pornography store, the man showed him an array of under-the-counter magazines and tapes offering more explicit and uncommon sexual activities. After purchasing several, Claude returned home with high hopes which, indeed, were fulfilled over the next few weeks. Again, though, he became bored with the sexual behaviours that he and his wife had practised over the years. He asked his wife to try one of the more unusual behaviours shown in the tapes; she did so reluctantly, and soon, he was pressuring her to try even more eccentric activities.

Over time, as Claude became more obsessed with pornography, his wife withdrew sexually from him. He exhausted his supply of local materials and began to write to out-of-country mail-order houses for increasingly bizarre materials. Finally, he purchased a videotape showing a man having sex with a girl about ten years old. Claude told the therapist that until he sent for this tape, he had entertained no thoughts of having sex with children. In fact, he said the notion previously would have repulsed him. The first time he watched the film, he felt aroused but confused. However, he masturbated while viewing it, and eventually, it began to excite him. Two months later, he tried to molest the babysitter.

It is clear that exposure to pornography exerts an

antisocial influence on a substantial proportion of males. These effects can range from the reinforcement of negative attitudes towards women and insensitivity to sexual assault of women and children to, in some cases, the evolution of deviant sexual tendencies. However, the proliferation of pornography is only one characteristic of a society that expresses insufficient respect for its women and children. The same patriarchal sentiments that support and dominate our burgeoning pornography industry help create and reinforce antiwoman and antichild images in advertising and other media. These male fantasies of life reflect the attitude that women and children are the property of men to do with as they wish. They also state that most women and children eagerly accept such positions as their rightful places. If we are serious about preventing sex offending, we must reconsider the thesis currently guiding all our media, both popular and pornographic.

It is hard to escape the conclusion that in a society free of oppressive attitudes, in which women were respected as the equals of men, and children were valued as whole but vulnerable individuals in need of encouragement and protection, there would not be any harmful media portrayals. Finally, although such a thing is difficult to imagine in our present world, there might not even be sex crimes. In the absence of any spontaneous groundswell in that direction, however, we support the current ban on depictions of violent sex and sex with children. Although the evidence with respect to degrading or impersonal sex seems strong, in our opinion it is not sufficiently extensive to warrant censorship. If further research confirms the findings to date, however, we would not hesitate to recommend banning these materials as well. On the other hand, since there is no indication of any negative effects caused by erotica, which depicts affectionate, enjoyable sexual relations between two consenting adults in positions of equal power, we see no reason to prohibit such materials simply because they are explicit.

The censorship of certain types of pornography does not seem to us to be such a dramatic curtailment of the freedom of a relative few when weighed against the harm it causes to the women and children affected by its message. While censorship is not without problems of definition, the same is true of all laws, which is why we have courts. It is worth noting here that an independent study conducted by Check found that more than 1,000 men from various walks of life could easily and correctly classify three different types of sexually explicit stimuli. All of these men saw one set of videotapes as forceful, a second as noncoercive but degrading, and a third set as affectionate, consenting and free of degradation. Apparently, it is easier to make these distinctions than some people believe.

But there is no point enacting legislation governing the production, distribution, and sale of pornography if police forces are not allocated adequate resources to vigorously enforce these laws. We urge all municipalities to recognize the threat that pictures and descriptions of violent sex and sex with children pose to a significant portion of their populations and to provide the manpower to ensure that such materials are not available in their communities. As long as we permit easy access to illegal pornography, we can never move past the short-term answers to the problems of sexual crimes.

10

The Case for Treatment

IN JUNE 1989, the chairman of the National Parole Board proposed a change in legislation governing federal prisoners. To end the frustration of correctional officials, Fred Gibson said, the board wanted to be able to keep all sex offenders in prison until the very last day of their sentences. His statement followed the widespread publicity surrounding two murders committed by sex offenders released on mandatory supervision after serving two-thirds of their prison terms. Applauded in some corners for its sentiment, Gibson's proposal was criticized in others for its lack of logic.

Sooner or later, the detractors pointed out, every inmate—with the exception of a relative few—will be released. The suggested change in legislation would not make the streets any safer: offenders who have served their entire sentences are under no supervision whatsoever when they are set free. The proposal would only relieve correctional authorities, particularly the parole board, of responsibility for a rapist or pedophile who reoffends while on parole or mandatory supervision.

"As long as we have a system of definite sentencing," says criminal lawyer David Cole, "they are getting out anyway. Sure, we can keep them in longer. We can say, 'Damn the costs of keeping them locked up.' But, ultimately, they are getting out."

Evidence collected over many years indicates that a substantial proportion of sex offenders who go untreated reoffend. According to official police files, thirty-five percent of untreated sex offenders released from Canadian prisons are reconvicted of a sexual offence; those with the longest records have the highest official recidivism rate. That figure, however, does not include rapists and child molesters who have committed new crimes but have not been charged or prosecuted. And as we have seen in previous chapters, there are many such cases.

When researchers from the Kingston Sexual Behaviour Clinic scrutinized unofficial files kept by police and children's aid societies, they found a different story. Over a four-year period, the rate of repeat offences for 126 child molesters assessed at the clinic was 2.5 times higher than was publicly acknowledged. The official recidivism for this particular group was seventeen percent; the actual rate, almost forty-three percent. Typically, the records showed that the men were not prosecuted because the victims were too young to give acceptable evidence or were considered unsatisfactory witnesses for some reason. Occasionally, however, either the offender was judged to be of such good character that charges were deemed unnecessary or, in the case of incest, it was felt that charges would do more damage to the family. Presumably, even the unofficial records underestimate the rate of repeat offences, since they rely on the victims both reporting the crimes and being able to identify the perpetrators.

On the basis of this 1988 study, it is reasonable to assume that the thirty-five percent official recidivism rate of untreated offenders released from prison is a marked underestimate. Clearly, incarceration alone is not effective in rehabilitating these men.

The toll in human suffering exacted by repeat offenders should be enough to convince the government to treat all sex offenders in prison and to provide follow-up treatment programs after they are released. It has not. Perhaps the financial costs will.

Researchers in both the United States and Canada have found that each time a sex offender reoffends, approximately $200,000 is spent investigating, prosecuting, incarcerating, and providing him with an assessment and minimal treatment in prison. This is a conservative vative figure based on an average police investigation, minimal court time and only one year's imprisonment. (The Canadian government calculated that each inmate cost the correctional system $42,695 in 1988.) The estimate also includes the cost of cursory treatment for the victim. Cases involving intensive police investigations would cost taxpayers considerably more; police in British Columbia, for example, spent at least $2.5 million in 1985 attempting to gather enough evidence to charge one serial rapist, according to lawyers connected with the case. Similarly, offences resulting in a trial by jury or in longer sentences would also significantly increase the expense.

If the same money was spent on a treatment program that prevented only one rapist or pedophile out of forty from reoffending, it would pay for itself. If the program stopped two sex offenders from committing new crimes, the government would save money. In considering the value of treatment, therefore, it is clear it does not have to be profoundly effective to be beneficial even in crass economic terms.

Cost-benefit ratios aside, some individuals argue that society should not spend any money treating sex offenders because they do not deserve it. Whether or not they do is irrelevant. Most sex offenders remain in the community. And those who are incarcerated eventually return. To ignore that reality is to place women and children at greater risk of being victimized.

Since attempting to treat sex offenders seems to be justified on both humane and economic grounds, it makes sense to examine the various forms of treatment and the relative effectiveness of each. Essentially, there are three approaches, each of which follows from one of three basic assumptions: that sex offenders have a physical abnormality; that their problems stem from their childhoods; or that their crimes are the product of a long history of learning that can be reversed.

According to the first perspective, sex offenders have a disturbance in the biochemical bases of sexual functioning. Their body stores of testosterone, or of other related sex steroids, are thought to be elevated. These hormones are believed to mediate, at least to some degree, the frequency and intensity of sexual desires and aggressive drives. There are few clinicians who would dismiss the role of sex steroids in the criminal behaviour of at least some sex offenders. But these men would appear to constitute only a small percentage of sex offenders as a whole.

At the Kingston clinic, for example, men who are found to have extremely high sex drives associated with strong aggressive tendencies are referred to a medical clinic that specializes in evaluating hormone levels. If tests confirm a hormonal imbalance, antiandrogen drugs are prescribed. In the past sixteen years, less than five percent of the Kingston clinic's patients have had to be referred for such treatment; therapy for the remaining ninety-five percent required no chemical intervention. Other clinics in North America also report that five percent or fewer of their patients require medication to correct a hormonal imbalance.

Drugs alone, however, are not considered by most clinicians to be an effective treatment for any sex offender. When they are prescribed, it is usually as an adjunct to psychiatric or psychological treatment, in the same way that tranquilizers might be recommended for an extremely agitated patient to allow him to relax enough to benefit from therapy. A treatment program conducted by John Bradford, a psychiatrist at the Royal Ottawa Hospital and one of the world's experts in evaluating and treating sex offenders with abnormal hormone levels, includes a wide range of behavioural and psychotherapeutic components. The purpose of the program is to teach patients to manage their lives so that they can eventually live offence-free without drugs.

An alternative, Draconian method of dealing with abnormal hormone levels is to castrate sex offenders. The procedure, which for ethical reasons is not used in Canada, involves removing the testes, the body's major centres for the production of testosterone. Castration does not completely prevent the manufacture of the hormone, nor does it eliminate all sexual activity. It does, however, permanently reduce the levels of testosterone in the bloodstream and significantly lower the patient's sex drive. There are a number of reports from Europe claiming successful treatment of sex offenders through castration, but the procedure has serious side-effects.

In 1968, for example, G.K. Sturup, a Danish social scientist, published the results of a long-term follow-up study of a group of castrated and noncastrated rapists. None of the castrated offenders had been reconvicted of a sexual crime, whereas ten percent of the control group had; however, thirty-three percent of the castrated rapists committed new nonsexual crimes, compared to only five percent of the controls. In 1978 and 1979, Nicholas Heim, a German psychologist, reported that castrated sex offenders are also more likely than their noncastrated counterparts to develop physical, psychiatric and social problems, and to become a liability to the state. It would appear, then, that while castration may satisfy a desire for vengeance, it is not an effective means of treating these men.

The second general type of treatment for sex offenders is based on traditional psychotherapy. A primary goal of these Freudian-based programs is to help the individual understand the origins of his criminal behaviour, which are usually thought to arise in his childhood, particularly through his relationship with his mother. Although disruptive childhoods are common in sex offenders, there does not seem to be any evidence that mothers play a crucial role in the development of sex offending. In fact, a study conducted in 1989 by Bill Pithers and his fellow psychologists at the Vermont Treatment Program for Sex Offenders suggests that neglect and abuse by fathers is more significant in the early development of sex offenders than any influence on the part of mothers.

The major flaw in the psychotherapeutic method, when practised in its traditional, or orthodox, form, is that it identifies a single problem as the origin of a sex offender's behaviour. Blaming his actions on his early childhood experiences, over which he had no control, also tends to relieve the offender of responsibility for his crimes. It further suggests that simply by gaining insight into the cause of his deviant behaviour, his problems will be solved. Few clinicians working with sex offenders today would accept such a premise. And, indeed, there are no longer many treatment programs based on this model.

By far the most common treatment for sex offenders

now—and the form that has been most carefully evaluated—is based on a cognitive-behavioural method. This approach assumes that sex offending is the result of a long history of social learning and has multiple causes. It takes the view that a sex offender not only has acquired negative skills during his lifetime—for example, how to force a woman or a child to have sex and minimize the chances of being caught—but that he is seriously deficient in a broad range of positive skills. He has acquired attitudes and behaviours that are antisocial and self-serving instead of beliefs that would allow him to feel confident, to function effectively, and to be dismayed by the use of aggression rather than utilize it to get his own way. The goal of these treatment programs is to reeducate sex offenders—to teach them new ways of thinking and behaving.

Cognitive-behavioural therapy considers that at least some sex offenders have developed a sexual attraction to forced sex or to sex with children. This theory does not deny that in the commission of rape, sex often plays a less significant role than aggression and degradation directed towards the victim; nor does it negate the satisfaction that child molesters gain from having power over their victims. These motives are addressed in therapy, as are social skills and life skills. Cognitive-behavioural therapy also attempts to instill in offenders empathy for their victims and to train them in relapse-prevention strategies. First, though, it deals with the offender's sexual behaviour.

Therapists begin by assessing, through the physiological testing process described earlier in this book, whether or not the man has deviant sexual proclivities. If he is attracted to consenting sex with an adult partner, his sexual preferences would not be a focus of his treatment program. If on the other hand he demonstrates the greatest arousal to, say, sex with children, attempts would be made to eliminate this inclination through two processes.

The first, known as covert sensitization, is designed to get the offender to link his deviant behaviour with its potential negative results. On one side of a card, which he is asked to carry with him and read daily, he describes his typical fantasy for sex offending; on the reverse, he lists what he fears will happen if he gets caught—he might lose his job, have his name published in the newspaper, go to prison, be beaten up by other inmates. . . . Eventually, every time he considers offending, he will automatically think of the possible consequences.

The second means of eliminating deviant proclivities is through masturbatory retraining. When they masturbate, offenders are asked to replace their fantasies of deviant sex with images of appropriate sexual behaviour. If they become aroused by thinking about forced sex, for instance, they are told to substitute thoughts of consenting sex before they ejaculate. Then, for at least twenty minutes immediately following orgasm, when they are disinterested in, or perhaps even repulsed by, sexual stimuli, they are asked to continue masturbating while describing aloud variations of their deviant fantasies.

In the early development of cognitive-behavioural programs, sexual preferences were considered to be the only area that needed to be addressed in treatment. There was a general consensus that all sex offenders must have deviant proclivities; if these were corrected, the men would cease offending. This theory is no longer accepted by most clinicians. At the Kingston Sexual Behaviour Clinic, deviant sexual preferences are regarded as a minor, although important, factor in the behaviour of offenders. As noted earlier, many rapists and child molesters do not have deviant preferences at all. In some outdated treatment programs, the absence of deviant preferences is taken to mean that the offender is not in need of treatment. This is a dangerous assumption. If a man has raped a woman or molested a child, he needs treatment whether he demonstrates deviant tendencies or not.

After assessing an offender's sexual preferences, cognitive-behavioural therapists evaluate his sexual comprehension. Here they are not so much interested in whether he knows the anatomy and physiology involved in sexual behaviour, but rather what his knowledge and attitudes are towards the full range of sexual behaviours that humans engage in when they are in a consenting and satisfactory sexual relationship. Many offenders, oddly enough, are particularly prudish in their attitudes towards sex. Many of them think that sex itself is disgusting. Even if they agree that some sexual interchanges are appropriate, they believe that the only acceptable form of intercourse is when the man is on top of the woman. Any variation in position or any form of foreplay is considered by them to be repugnant, despite the fact that they may express a desire to participate in these acts. For example, although anal intercourse is a common feature of rape, many rapists perceive it to be a repulsive activity.

In some as yet unclear manner, the prudishness of sex offenders seems to be related to their crimes. This, of course, does not mean that all men who are sexual prudes will become sex offenders. But it does suggest that for some offenders, prudish attitudes hinder their participation in normal adult sexual relationships and, in turn, may help drive them to their offensive behaviours.

Sex offenders usually change the way they view certain sexual practices when they are given evidence of the incidence of such behaviour and the satisfaction it produces among normal well-functioning members of society. In a group therapy session, a therapist will ask offenders to explain what they think is wrong with various sexual acts. Typically they say, "everyone thinks it is awful," at which point the therapist can present data to challenge this notion.

Many offenders also fail to recognize the different needs they are attempting to satisfy through sex; they identify orgasm alone as their goal. Again, a number of men in the nonoffending community focus simply on physical gratification in sexual activity. But just because offenders share this characteristic with nonoffenders does not mean it is irrelevant to treatment. Many alcoholics are socially anxious and use alcohol as a way of reducing anxiety. The fact that many nonalcoholics are also socially anxious does not mean that therapists ignore anxiety when treating addiction.

Cognitive-behavioural therapists help offenders to recognize that power, aggression, and degradation of victims are important aspects of sexual offences but that they are not ordinarily pursued in healthy sexual relationships. They point out, as well, that sexual interchanges can satisfy a wide range of common needs, such as the need for affection and intimacy, for confirmation of a partner's love, for a sense of masculinity, and for relief from anxiety or despair. Once offenders understand their own needs, they can try to develop ways of meeting them in the context of an affectionate, intimate relationship with a consenting adult partner. This aspect of treatment also helps them to see that pursuing sex or power as exclusive goals with inappropriate or unwilling partners will never fully satisfy them and will only lead to an escalation in their offensive behaviours.

Finally, within the sexual domain, therapists determine whether there is any sexual dysfunction contributing to the offender's behaviour. Some older men who molest children, for example, are impotent. This presents a serious threat to their masculinity, which is reinforced whenever they fail in an attempt to have sex with acceptable partners. They therefore turn to children, who do not know a man is supposed to have an erection. These men participate in the full sex offender program but are also referred to a centre that specializes in treating impotence.

Social skills are targeted second in cognitive-behavioural programs. The emphasis is on teaching socially inept offenders adequate interpersonal skills and on reducing their anxiety about social interactions, particularly with adult females. There are two reasons for this component. First, if an offender is unable to get involved in an intimate relationship with an appropriate partner, he will be more likely to continue to seek sexual satisfaction through forced sex or sex with children. Second, deficient social skills can create stress, and there is ample evidence that stress increases the likelihood of any regressive behaviour, including sex offending.

At the Kingston clinic, female university student volunteers are sometimes recruited to participate in role-playing exercises with sex offenders who have difficulty in either initiating or carrying on a conversation with a woman. Under the direction of a therapist, the student and the offender might pretend that they have just met at a party. Some offenders have no trouble starting or continuing a conversation; they may have relationships with women but are unable to get beyond a superficial level of interaction. These men, too, are encouraged to rehearse various conversations in therapy sessions and to try them out later with their actual partners.

Stress management is incorporated into the life-skills aspect of the program. Offenders are taught how to reduce anxiety by avoiding confrontational issues and by arranging their lives so that they are not working to the point of exhaustion or taking on the responsibilities of other people. Participants are also taught how to deal with stress when it cannot be avoided. Faced with an inevitable marital breakdown, for instance, an offender is counselled that there is nothing he can do to control the situation and he will only feel greater stress if he tries.

Since rapists and child molesters are also at risk of reoffending when they are bored or spend a lot of time alone, they are taught constructive ways to spend their spare time and how to integrate such periods into their relationships with partners or friends. If they have difficulty with alcohol, they are trained to use the drug moderately as well as to manage their behaviour when they are intoxicated.

The distorted attitudes and beliefs that support continued sex offending are targeted next. Many rapists, as we have seen, believe that women have a secret desire to be raped. And many child molesters see children as seductive and as suffering no harm as a result of sex with adults. Whether these attitudes were present before they committed their sex crimes or arose as a means of justifying their behaviour is irrelevant. As outlined in the previous chapter, aggression studies have shown that the more the aggressor views his victims as different from him, the easier it is to hurt them. Therefore, training perpetrators to be empathetic towards their victims—to see them as human beings with the same feelings and needs as they have—is crucial. The offenders are given a detailed account of the harm that results from sex offending and are frequently either shown videotapes of victims recounting their distress or are confronted with an actual victim.

Finally, offenders are trained in relapse-prevention strategies. A distinction is made between lapses, which are the precursors to offending, and relapses. A lapse occurs when an offender has thoughts of offending or entertains masturbatory fantasies about raping a woman or molesting a child; he may also daydream about gaining access to a victim. A relapse is when a man acts on these thoughts or fantasies, when he puts his plan into action and actually offends. Pithers and his former colleague Janice Marques developed this relapse-prevention approach from the work of Seattle psychologist Alan Marlatt, who is one of North America's foremost specialists in the treatment of addictions. It is designed to maintain the positive changes produced by treatment so that the temptations and difficulties encountered in everyday life will not lead an offender to commit another crime.

Patients are told that lapses do not indicate failure. They are to be expected and can be used as a basis for learning how to control the problem better. The premise is that a man who sees a lapse as a failure will define himself that way and feel depressed; he will see himself as a sex offender who cannot control himself and will give in to the temptation to reoffend. If he further interprets a lapse as an indication that he has not profited from treatment, the push to reoffend will be even greater.

In this part of the program, patients are taught how to recognize high risk situations, to avoid them where possible, and deal with them where necessary. Offenders learn to discern the sequence of thoughts and behaviours that lead to trouble and to interrupt this process at an early point. If a child molester waits until he is alone with a child before he attempts to control himself, then obviously, he will have far more difficulty than if he stopped himself when he first thought about going to a place where he knew there would be a lot of children. Many offenders make decisions that appear on the surface to be unrelated to the issue of sexual assault but lead to it. A rapist may feel bored and decide that, since it is a nice day, he will go for a drive. If this man has typically attacked hitchhikers, his decision to go for a drive is not insignificant, even if he has convinced himself that he is not thinking about offending.

Sometimes sex offenders engage in passive planning in which they allow events to unfold in a way that provides access to a victim. One child molester told his therapist that it was not his fault that his wife and her friend asked him to babysit the friend's eleven year old daughter while they went shopping. Closer analysis of the sequence of events showed, however, that he had felt attracted to this young girl several times in the past. He recognized early in the day that if they were all to have dinner together, the two women would have to buy groceries and would probably ask him to stay with the young girl. He suggested that the friend stay for dinner and then let things take their course.

In the period immediately prior to their crimes, sex offenders respond to their needs for immediate gratification without concern for the long-term consequences. Often, there is little alternative satisfaction in their lives; they use sex, and particularly sex offences, to cheer themselves up when they are low or stressed or when they want to relieve their feelings of deprivation. By learning new ways of thinking and behaving, they can interrupt the offending process and substitute a socially acceptable and gratifying behaviour during these times. Men at risk might indulge a sweet tooth with a chocolate éclair, for example, or relax by going for a run or playing a game of tennis, or work on a household project. They are also taught that they should not expect to be rewarded every time they feel deprived; they can tolerate the experience if they stop feeling sorry for themselves.

The effectiveness of cognitive-behavioural treatment programs can be expected to vary, depending on the circumstances of operation. The major drawback to such programs in prisons is the fact that they do not involve a gradual assimilation of the offender back into the community with appropriate supervision and follow-up treatment. Nonetheless, even when the programs are conducted in secure institutional settings under less than optimal conditions, they have resulted in lower reoffence rates.

One exception to this general rule was reported in 1989 by researchers at the Oakridge Mental Health Centre in Penetanguishene. They found that thirty-seven percent of a treated group of 136 sex offenders committed new sexual crimes, compared to thirty-one percent of an untreated group. The most apparent reason for the failure of this group of offenders is the fact that ninety-four of them received only aversive therapy. Mildly uncomfortable shocks were administered to their forearms as they watched slides of deviant sexual activity. Another forty-two also received some social skills training but nothing else. Most clinicians would not consider this program to be adequate in any setting, and Oakridge's is far from ideal.

The centre primarily houses criminally insane patients, including some extremely dangerous sex offenders, in overcrowded quarters in an old building on the shores of Georgian Bay in central Ontario. Patients in the treatment program live with other men who are similarly disturbed but untreated, many of whom spend a lot of time communicating their aberrant sexual fantasies to one another. This creates pressure on the treated inmates to return to their deviant ways of thinking. The negative influence is exacerbated by the fact that the treated offenders are not released for months or even years after they have finished the program. And finally, like many other inpatient treatment programs of this kind, the men are not required to enter any follow-up program when they are back in the community. Under the circumstances, it is not surprising that researchers found this program to be ineffective.

Some bureaucrats who are tired of trying to meet public demands for proper protection from sex offenders have implied that the lack of success at Oakridge means that sex offenders are generally untreatable. But this conclusion flies in the face of a solid body of evidence to the contrary. Many studies across North America confirm that treatment reduces the rate of recidivism among sex offenders.

Barry Maletzky, a psychiatrist in Portland, Oregon, examined the official records of 1,719 treated sex offenders over a fourteen-year period. He found that only 5.5 percent had committed new sex crimes.

When researchers at the Kingston clinic scrutinized the unofficial records of a group of 126 offenders, they found that treatment had reduced the rate of actual repeat offences among the offenders to thirteen percent from thirty-five percent. (Therapy had the greatest effect on men who molested boys: the recidivism rate among the treated offenders in this group was thirteen percent, compared to forty-three percent in the untreated group. Treatment reduced the reoffence rate among men who molested girls to eighteen percent from forty-three percent, and among incest offenders to eight percent from twenty-two percent.)

Researchers followed offenders for an average of four years. During that time, the treated offenders were compared with a matched group of untreated offenders in terms of the number and age of their previous victims, the amount of violence in their crimes, the length of their offence histories, as well as personal characteristics such as age, intelligence, and socioeconomic status. Both the treated and untreated groups had been assessed at the clinic, had admitted their offences, and had wanted treatment. (The second group did not receive treatment primarily because the offenders lived too far away to attend on a regular basis. The men were, however, referred to counsellors closer to their own communities; so in a sense, they are not accurately described as untreated, although any therapy received was not as comprehensive as that provided by the program at the Kingston clinic.)

The results of the study show that the reoffence rate among men who molested other people's daughters was twenty-five percent lower in the treated group than in the untreated group, indicating that of every one hundred men treated at the Kingston clinic, twenty-five would have committed other sex crimes if they had been left untreated. Since the untreated child molesters who did reoffend averaged two victims each, we can assume that about fifty children were saved from becoming victims. Furthermore, since it costs the government about $200,000 for each convicted repeat offender, we can extrapolate that it would save twenty-five times that amount, or more than $5 million, over the two years it takes the clinic to treat one hundred offenders. (During a two-year period, the program itself receives only $120,000 in provincial government grants.)

Research has indicated that treatment for rapists and exhibitionists is not quite as effective as it is with child molesters. Nevertheless, similar discrepancies between the reoffence rate among treated and untreated offenders have been shown, and the subsequent savings to society, again, are substantial.

In all major cities in Canada and in many smaller centres, there are community treatment clinics staffed by clinicians experienced in treating sex offenders. Most of these clinics would happily accept ex-inmates referred by Canadian prisons if only the federal government would pay for such treatment.

Treatment alone is not enough, however. It is crucial to keep sex offenders under some form of scrutiny for some time after therapy. Treated rapists and child molesters are in a position much like treated alcoholics. Even if an alcoholic was considered to be effectively treated, no responsible clinician would recommend that he accept a job as a bartender. Similarly, an ex-sex offender should never be allowed to be in a position where he has easy power over women or ready access to children. Research conducted at various treatment centres around the world has consistently shown that when child molesters reoffend, it is because they have been in high risk situations—alone with children of their preferred age and gender. This point is particularly salient in the current Canadian context where a number of male Catholic clergy have been convicted of sexually abusing altar boys. A newspaper article about one of these cases reported that the Church was prepared to accept the man back into the role of parish priest if he were shown to be rehabilitated. This would put him back into the same circumstances as those which surrounded his original offence. Obviously, this is an unwise strategy. Even if these offenders are treated, they are not "cured," and they should not be allowed to resume their positions as parish priests. The same is true for many other professionals such as teachers, doctors, and lawyers.

Treatment for sex offending is not like a vaccine against polio or the measles. It does not eliminate the possibility of the behaviour occurring again. It simply reduces the chances that it will recur. While treatment is clearly beneficial to most patients, some sex offenders reoffend even after going through a comprehensive and thorough program from which they appeared to have benefited, although typically, they will reoffend against fewer victims than untreated offenders.

When researchers at the Kingston clinic examined the factors that might predict reoffending, two stood out: younger offenders appeared less likely to benefit from treatment than older offenders; and child molesters who had simulated, attempted or actually had intercourse with their victims were at higher risk of reoffending than those who had not.

Treatment is effective, but it is not a permanent

cure and it is not successful in every case. This does not mean, however, that we should abandon our attempts to treat difficult patients, who may be among the most dangerous. Rather, it indicates that we should work hard at developing a better understanding of why current treatment fails with these men so that we can produce a program that will be more effective.

We have really just begun the process of treating sex offenders in a comprehensive fashion and carefully evaluating the results. Modern cognitive-behavioural treatment programs, which include all of the components described in this chapter, have been in effect for only a decade. And the difficulty clinicians have experienced in obtaining government monies to operate these programs has been surpassed only by the resistance they have encountered trying to get grants to evaluate them. We need to know a lot more. The only viable method is to deliver treatment to all offenders and to conduct long-term outcome studies to determine the results.

11

Beyond the Short-term Answers

CHILD-CARE WORKERS responded with guarded optimism when the Newfoundland government promised in the spring of 1989 to launch an inquiry into the sexual abuse of children by clergy and lay members of the Roman Catholic Church. "We'd be delighted if [the task force] would look at what needs to be done," one professional told the media. "I don't think they need to spend any time on whether or not a problem exists. They can take it for granted that a problem exists."

It was a comment that could apply equally to the sexual assault of women and to the handling of sex offenders themselves. Countless royal commissions, public inquests, and internal government investigations have identified the cracks in the system. It is time to start mending them. If the millions of taxpayers' dollars spent reconfirming the problems were reallocated to solutions, the incidence of sexual crimes could be drastically reduced.

In the previous chapter, we outlined not just the benefits but the necessity of treating sex offenders. The context in which therapy is offered is equally important. Treatment should be provided to all incarcerated rapists and pedophiles early in their sentences, when the motivation to change is the highest. When sex offenders are forced to wait for years for treatment—as currently happens (if they are treated at all)—their hope and enthusiasm dissolve into cynicism and despair. Since their crimes are loathed as much by other inmates as they are by society in general, these offenders become secretive about their offences and are reluctant to discuss them when and if they finally do enter therapy; the delay also entrenches their tendency to diminish and rationalize what they have done. Furthermore, by living in the general prison population, sex offenders learn to do only what is absolutely necessary to meet some clearly defined rules. These attitudes are not conducive to effective treatment.

Ideally, in addition to going through a comprehensive treatment program when they first enter prison, sex offenders should remain in some form of therapeutic environment for the duration of their sentences so that the gains they have made through therapy will not be lost. A separate federal penitentiary for rapists and child molesters could provide such an atmosphere and would make it easier for these inmates to participate in additional treatment sessions periodically throughout their incarceration—a process that has been shown to reduce even further the risk of recidivism.

The current situation in which sex offenders are mixed with "solid" criminals in prisons understandably creates a "security first; treatment second" approach to their incarceration. A separate federal penitentiary for rapists and child molesters would eliminate many security problems and would allow a reversal of the security first attitude. Presumably, it would also save money now spent protecting sex offenders from other inmates. All staff in such an institution could be trained in both therapeutic management and security procedures.

Finally, a single prison for sex offenders would likely reduce errors in release decisions. All of the information on each inmate—criminal records and reports by penitentiary case management workers, security officers, and treatment and psychiatric staff—would be in the same location, readily accessible to parole officers and the parole board. The staff themselves would be better informed about the inmates and in a better position to work together, rather than at cross purposes, which so often happens now. And as part of a team, individual staff members would be less vulnerable to being manipulated by an inmate into feeling solely responsible for his fate and, as a result, would be less likely to recommend inappropriate releases. Decisions could be made collectively and presented to the inmates as such. In the case of the most dangerous offenders, independent outside psychiatric or psychological evaluations should still be sought before an inmate is let out.

Treating rapists and pedophiles in prison is not enough, however. The federal government must accept responsibility for the sex offenders it releases into the community. These inmates should be gradually reintegrated into society under the close supervision of specially trained parole supervisors. In Vermont, the correctional service has achieved remarkable success with a program introduced by Bill Pithers, a psychologist, in which parole officers are taught to recognize indications of potential relapse in paroled sex offenders. The officers are also trained to assist these offenders to steer clear of risky situations and to deal with them when they are unavoidable.

Every sex offender released from prison should also have an individual plan for follow-up treatment, paid for by the federal government. All major Canadian cities and many smaller ones have community treatment centres staffed by clinicians experienced in treating sex offenders. Most would gladly accept ex-prisoners if they were paid. Apparently, however, these centres have met the same bureaucratic obstacles as the Kingston Sexual Behaviour Clinic, which assesses more than two hundred sex offenders annually and treats more than fifty. Although the clinic has offered on numerous occasions to provide treatment for sex offenders who are released from federal penitentiaries in Ontario, the Canadian government has not taken advantage of its services. At the provincial government level, the Ontario Ministry of Health has acknowledged the value of the clinic's treatment program but has concluded that sex offending is not a mental health problem. The Ontario Ministry of Community and Social Services terminated its funding for the clinic—in spite of the fact that many of its patients are referred by children's aid societies— because most of these individuals are adults and the ministry is responsible only for juvenile offenders; at the same time, it recognized that the program was preventing future sexual crimes against children. Only the support of the Ontario Ministry of Correctional Services has allowed the clinic to remain in operation. For the entire 1989–90 fiscal year, the ministry provided $60,000, which pays the salaries of two staff. Marshall and Howard Barbaree, the co-directors, donate their time.

The federal government is placing women and children at greater risk of being victimized by failing to treat all rapists and child molesters in prison or to provide adequate supervision and follow-up treatment for the sex offenders it releases from penitentiaries. To imply, as at least one senior member of the correctional service has, that nothing could have been done to prevent the tragic crimes perpetrated in recent years by sex offenders fresh out of prison suggests a complacency that only men—who are rarely the victims of sexual assault—could possibly feel. While it *may* be impossible to eliminate all errors, every conceivable attempt must be made to reduce them to as near zero as possible. Any effort of this kind has yet to be demonstrated.

While the federal government neglects the treatment needs of many convicted sex offenders—in fact, it appears that the primary purpose of existing treatment is to appease the public in the wake of controversy—the provincial governments provide only token support for the victims of sexual assault. There is no systematic approach to the design, funding, and implementation of such services across the country. Even within individual provinces, there is great disparity from one region to another. Staff shortages at child protection agencies and child mental health centres mean that children can wait for months before complaints of sexual abuse are even investigated and then many more months before counselling is received. Where rape crisis centres and shelters for women and children exist, operated by private groups with government grants, they are in constant jeopardy of having to shut down because of insufficient funds from the provincial governments. Indeed, many have closed. And if it were not for the courage and energy of the staff and volunteers, there would be very few centres still in existence.

Providing the financial resources to treat offenders and to support victims is just the beginning. There must be a fundamental change in the way that sexual crimes are viewed by the professionals who deal with them and by society in general.

When a victim reports an assault, it is imperative that everyone involved take the incident seriously, regardless of who is being accused, whether or not he is known to the victim, and how respectable he may appear. The individual who first receives the complaint, the police who investigate it, and the friends and family of the victim must all respond supportively: they must accept, until there is clear evidence to the contrary, that what the victim says is true; they must indicate clearly that the victim is not at fault in any way; and they must aid the victim in pursuing the complaint.

Too often, victims are treated as though they, rather than the alleged offenders, are the subjects of investigation. We do not expect men to be careful, for example, about how much they drink or about going out alone at night. Yet, if a women does this and is raped, she is held responsible. If a child is sexually assaulted while playing alone, we criticize the mother for being neglectful. We must stop blaming the victims.

Similarly, child protection agencies must end the practice of removing victims from their homes in cases of incest while allowing the perpetrators to remain. This policy revictimizes the child and, again, conveys the message that it is he or she who has done something wrong.

Until victims can be confident that their complaints will be dealt with seriously and sensitively, most will continue to keep them secret. When sexual crimes are not reported, the offender is given the clear message that he can continue to assault with impunity.

When victims first lodge their complaints—long before reaching the courts—they should be provided with an advocate who will accompany them throughout the entire judicial process. While the staff of sexual assault crisis centres have attempted to play this role, severe funding constraints have made universal assistance increasingly difficult. Crisis centres should be granted sufficient money to offer every victim an advocate who understands the entire system, from what happens during the standard medical examination for rape victims (many women do not know, for example, that the clothing they were wearing during the attack will be retained as evidence) to courtroom procedures.

Since the responses of those involved with victims of sexual assault are usually based on their ignorance of the nature of the crime, its perpetrators, and its effects, special training should be provided for all police officers who deal with sexual assault cases. Such programs should be designed by objective experts and be comprehensive and ongoing; they should debunk the myths about rape and child molestation, outline the true extent and nature of these crimes, explain the range of possible reactions by victims of sexual assault, and perhaps most important, emphasize that sex offenders come from every walk of life. Sexual assault education courses (a few have already been established) cannot be effective, however, unless they are assigned high priority and are genuinely supported by the most senior staff of individual police forces.

Clearly, many judges also have little understanding of sexual crimes. They need to be educated. And to eliminate the wide disparity in the punishments judges mete out to sex offenders, the federal government should provide the judiciary with detailed sentencing guidelines calling on them to justify any deviation from the directives. While judges obviously have to be allowed some discretion in their decisions, discretionary power is now so great that it invites the introduction of personal bias.

Physicians and other health professionals, as well as social workers, teachers, and day-care workers, should be well educated in the signs of child molestation. A family physician in eastern Ontario recently told a

forum on sexual assault that she did not see a single
victim of incest during her first seven years of practice;
after she attended an in-depth conference on the subject and became aware of the symptoms, she was
shocked by how many cases she came across.

The absurdly formal nature of our courts and their
adversarial structure is inappropriate in dealing with
crimes of sexual assault, especially against children.
Courtrooms, with their severe and stern aura, threaten
even some of the experienced professionals who are
called as expert witnesses. Imagine how intimidating
they must be for children. Is it necessary for judges and
lawyers in child abuse cases to wear robes and for
judges to sit in elevated positions?

Cross examination of victims is often offensive and
counterproductive in elucidating the facts in the cases.
The underlying assumption of the court seems to be
that war is the only way to peace. Defence lawyers
often attack witnesses in an insulting and belligerent
manner. Indeed, the most successful and admired lawyers are those who are most able to upset and confuse
witnesses. This confrontational style, which can interfere with an individual's ability to recall accurately
pertinent information and to relate this evidence in a
credible fashion, does not serve the best interests of
justice. The legal system should be encouraged to
de-emphasize the importance of the debating skills of
lawyers in determining whether an alleged sex offender
is innocent or guilty and adopt a format that concen-
trates on the illumination of facts. It should also endeavour,
wherever possible, to avoid bringing children into the
courtroom, where they may be intimidated and further
traumatized by having to testify in front of their assailants. Instead, children should be permitted to give
their testimony during videotaped or live remote-camera
interviews conducted by objective but sympathetic individuals appointed by the court.

An adversarial system, which by necessity pits would-be winners against one another, is unlikely to secure justice. It has little room for human compassion. It is no wonder that defendants and plaintiffs alike feel cheated and unrecognized in such a system. More informality and greater genuine access to the process on the part of the real protagonists, not just their lawyers, would help the participants feel that true justice was being done. And it probably would be.

The attitudes that contribute to the miscarriage of justice in cases of sexual assault do not exist in isolation. They are systemic. They arise not from the bizarre reasoning of a few misguided people or extremists, but from the general context of a society that protects men and relegates women and children to the status of second-class citizens. While we have to ferret out injustice and incompetence within the criminal justice system and the penal-parole system, we must also address the underlying roots of sexual assault within our patriarchal society—a society that applauds aggression, promotes negative views of women, and does not properly value children.

Studies by Peggy Sanday, an American anthropologist, of more than one hundred primitive societies have demonstrated a clear link between patriarchal values and a high incidence of rape. Societies in which warfare was rare, in which men and women shared political, social, and economic power, and in which children were important had low rates of sexual assault. If patriarchal attitudes are at the root of sexual crimes, anything that helps eliminate these values should also reduce the frequency of such crimes.

Sex offenders prey on the vulnerability of women and children. When women have equal power, they will not be as defenceless. Beyond the short-term solutions, we must work towards creating a society that is genuinely egalitarian with respect to gender. Women must have the same access as men to political, social, and economic power. Laws and constitutional amendments that eradicate prejudice against women are necessary steps. But these goals will not be achieved by simple decree. As we have seen, not only pornography but much of the general media's presentation of men and women instils a negative view of women. Unless these messages are changed, legislative change will have little effect.

The media must begin to accept responsibility for the material it presents. It must start to monitor itself. Aggression is almost a constant feature of North American television, film, rock music, cartoons, and comics. Worse, violence is often fused with sexuality and contempt for women. When children are inundated with these messages day after day, their attitudes are moulded in a manner that makes them more vulnerable to the extended lies of pornography. If we are to create a more peaceful, gentle society, violence must be seen as destructive, not as a successful solution to problems. Titillation and disrespect for women and children have to give way to more appropriate forms of entertainment. Women must be portrayed in a realistic and positive fashion; relations between men and women must be depicted in healthy ways.

Our educational and child-rearing practices also need to be changed. Boys must learn that men can be happy and successful without being aggressive. In fact, aggression and its corollary, extreme competitiveness, seem to be decidedly incompatible with happiness and contentment, although they may at present further the acquisition of material wealth. Similarly, if girls are encouraged always to be passive and submissive, it is less likely that they will live fulfilled lives.

All children should be emboldened with self-confidence. Many children are vulnerable to sex offenders because they have been taught not to question adults;

child molesters rely on this vulnerability. Some parents also seem reluctant to compliment their children's successes for fear they will become prideful or arrogant. Yet self-confidence can allow children to reject the advances of some molesters because they recognize they have rights over their own bodies. Furthermore, self-confident children do not need the attention that certain child molesters bestow. If children are also taught to trust their own feelings, they may be more likely to stay away from individuals who make them feel uncomfortable. Nurturing a sense of self-love in children could also eliminate a child's later need to exercise power over others, one of the factors that can lead to sex offending. Teachers could enhance these processes by ensuring that their students are applauded for every achievement, both large and small.

Schools can educate children about the realities of sexual abuse, underlining how widespread the problem is and that the victims are never at fault, while providing them with a specially trained counsellor in whom they can confide at any time. The curriculum can also be designed to promote healthy attitudes towards human sexual relationships. In 1989 James Check, a researcher at York University in Toronto, studied the attitudes of high school students towards sexuality. His subsequent report emphasized the need for better sex education: "At present, all too many sex education classes in Canada focus on what might be termed the plumbing aspects of human sexuality and largely ignore the critically important social and behavioural aspects of sexual intimacy.

"Children are not presented with models of positive, affectionate, realistic sexual behaviour as part of their sex education in the schools. In fact, it may very well be that with the rapid expansion and use of videotapes, these students learn about the social and behavioural aspects of human sexuality from pornogra-

phy. In the absence of educational information to coun-
teract the frequently misleading and false messages in
pornography, is it any wonder that our young people
believe that force, sexual coercion, and adversarial
approaches to sexual behaviour are acceptable and perhaps even the norm?... Isn't it about time we taught
our children that women do not enjoy being raped, and
that, in fact, men and women are not adversaries in the
sexual arena?... Such a social sex education curriculum
is not only critically needed but long overdue."

Recent events in Newfoundland have highlighted
the fact that sexual crimes are a devastating social
problem. Canadians must convince the highest levels of
government that they consider women and children to
be important members of society and that they want
this very real threat to their lives to be expunged. To
spend more public money on inquiries or even on
victim-awareness campaigns is pointless without funding
resources that can actually help the problem. While
the solutions are not without cost, this expenditure
will be more than justified by the long-term savings it
will effect in both financial and human terms. The
problem of sexual crimes cannot be solved by politicians alone, however. It cannot be eradicated, either,
solely by professionals who treat offenders or support
victims.

A society that permits public expressions of contempt for women can only expect that women will be
victimized. A society that keeps children in ignorance
and in unquestioning obedience to adults cannot hope
that they will not be abused. Nor can such a society
expect that the administrators of justice will deal in an
appropriate manner with the men who sexually assault
women and children. Only if each of us has a deep-
seated change of heart and makes a long-term commitment to changing our attitudes and behaviours will the
problem finally be addressed and solved.

Notes

Chapter Three: Behind the Walls

The General Program for the Development of Psychiatric Services in the Federal Correctional Services in Canada (1973).

The quotes from the federal-provincial working group came from *The Management and Treatment of Sex Offenders, Report of the Working Group, Sex Offender Treatment Review* (1989).

Chapter Four: The Profile of a Sex Offender

Wherever first names only are used in this chapter (or elsewhere in the book), they are pseudonyms.

Chapter Six: Shattering the Myths

The Badgley stats are taken from the report, *Sexual Offences Against Children*, vol. 1 (1984).

Chapter Nine: The Link to Pornography

More information is available from the following sources:

The U.S. Attorney General's Commission on Pornography (July 1986), *Final Report*. Washington, D.C.: The U.S. Department of Justice.

Pornography: Research Advances and Policy Considerations, edited by Dolf Zillmann and Jennings Bryant. (Hillsdale, New Jersey: Lawrence Erlbaum Associates, Inc., 1989).

The Role of Pornography in Woman Abuse, Patricia Harmon and James Check. (Toronto: York University, 1989).

Pornography and Sexual Aggression, edited by Neil Malamuth and Edward Donnerstein. (New York: Academic Press, 1984).

Chapter Ten: The Case for Treatment

More information on issues related to the treatment of sex offenders can be found in *Handbook of Sexual Assault: Issues, Theories, and Treatment of the Offender*, edited by W.L. Marshall, D.R. Laws, and H.E. Barbaree. (New York: Plenum Press, 1990).

Index

A

Abbotsford treatment centre, 52, 53
Abel, Gene, 156–157, 172
Accused, The, 149
adversarial court system and sexual assault cases, 205–206
Albert, child molester, 91–92
Alberta Hospital, 14–15
Archambault prison, 31
Askey, Alan, 18
Attorney General's Commission on Pornography, 173
aversion treatment, 54

B

Badgley, Robin, 142
Badgley parliamentary committee, 109–110
Baird, Carol, 120
Bandura, Albert, 165, 168
Barbaree, Howard, 9, 95, 201
and Kingston Sexual Behaviour Clinic, 53
Barnes, Douglas, 37–38

Beatty, Perrin, 28
Beaver Creek, 53
Bennett, Ross, 22, 24, 28–29
Benson, Pam, 107–108, 116, 145–150, 152
Bird, Bruce, 34
Boden, Wayne, 41
Boston City Hospital, 114
Bourassa, Robert, 141
Bowden Institution, 41
Bradford, John, 183
Brian, child molester, 74–75
Bryant, Jennings, 168, 169
Bundy, Ted, 79–80, 82, 132, 154–155
Burt, Martha, 111

C

Campbell, Bishop Colin, 121, 126
Canadian Coalition Against Media Pornography, 162
Canadian Judicial Council, 136
Cannon, Robert, and Melvin Stanton, 16
Carstairs, Sharon, 137
castration of sex offenders, 183–184

Check, James, 110, 165–166, 178, 208–209

child molesters, 1–9, 70, 100–101
  Albert, 91–92
  Brian, 74–75
  Claude, 175–176
  Fredericks, Joseph, 34–35
  Gary, 72–74
  Gordon, 83
  Graham, 68–72
  Jim, 98–99
  Jones, James Patrick, 156
  Kocurek, Paul, 29–30
  Noyes, Robert, 85–90, 123–124
  Olson, Clifford, 79–80
  Peter, 98
  Reid, Peter, 124
  Ron, 101–102
  Taylor, Duane, 1–9, 80–81
  Warren, 76–78
  see also individual names
  infant abuse, 113–114
  Mount Cashel orphanage, 79
  profile of, 68–84, 85–106
  recidivism rate, 180–181
child sexual abuse, as major
    social problem, 141–142
children:
  and the courts, 205
  and pornography, 169–170
Children's Aid Society, 123
Christian Brothers, 79, 118–119
Clarke Institute of Psychiatry, 11,
    57, 93, 172
Claude, child molester, 175–176
cognitive-behavioural therapy,
    185–188, 192–193
Cole, David, 28, 37, 57, 60, 180
Coleman, James, 82
community residential centres *see*
    halfway houses
computer testing, 49–52, 70–71,
    77, 93

Conacher, Neil, 10–11
Connors, Darren, 139–140
Conter, Tema, 10, 13, 22–24, 27,
    28
  csc investigation, 63
  inquest, 16
conviction rates, 108–109
Correctional Service of Canada
    (csc), 28
  and internal inquiry, 8
  parole service, 26
  and politics, 40–41
Corrigan, John, 121
cost of crime, 35, 181–182
Court, John, 171–172
Cowart, Judge Edward, 132
criminal justice system, 22–25
Crosbie, Douglas, 11

D

Dan, child molester, 102
D'Arcy Development Centre, 5
Darke, Juliet, 97–98
Devine, Brendan, 140
Dobson, David, and
    pornography, 156
Dobson, James, 154–155
Dorran, B.W.M., 15
Drumheller Institution, 14
Duffett, Pauline, 143–144
Dynasty, 158

E

Earle, Shane, 120, 122
erotica, 177–178
  definition of, 157–158
Evans, Ross, 38–39
Evraire, Paul, 28

F

Fauteaux Report, 63
Federal Business Development
    Bank, and strip clubs funding,
    144
Ferguson, Simonne, 12–13
Finkelhor, David, 116
Fletcher, Robert, 32
Florida State Prison, 154
Foster, Allan George, 20
Fowler, James, 41
Fredericks, Joseph, 34–35
Fred, rapist, 95–96
Freudian theory of sexual
    offenders, 96–97
Freund, Kurt, 93

G

Gary, child molester, 72–74
gating, 4
Gibson, Fred, 179
Gingras, Daniel, 33–34, 40–41
Globe and Mail, 139, 144–145
Goldstein, Michael, 173
"good of the offender", 27–28
Gordon, child molester, 83
Graham, child molester, 68–72
Gratton, Michel, 141
Groth, Nicholas, 94–95, 113, 115
Guess? jeans advertisement, 158

H

habitual sex offenders, 22
Hackett, Donna, 137–138
halfway houses, 4, 5
handwriting analysis, 33
Haroun, Ellen, 126
health insurance, provision of to
    inmates, 11
Health and Welfare Canada,

family violence-prevention
    division, 142
Heim, Nicholas, 184
Henry, Dale, 129
Hickey, Reverend James, 83, 121
Hinch, Ronald, 127
homosexual pedophile, 87–90
Horizon House, 6, 12
Huyghebaert, Andre, 56–62

I

incest:
    and child protection agencies,
      203
    effect on victims, 146–151
    offenders, 82, 98, 99, 100
    Jeff, offender, 104
    victims and the courts, 142–143
infant abuse, 113–114, 140–141

J

James, Bruce John, 33
James, Judge A.F., 18–19
Jeff, incest offender, 104
Jim, child molester, 98–99
John Howard Society, 25
    and parole system
      recommendations, 42–43
Jones, James Patrick, and
      pornography, 156
judges, and attitudes to sexual
      assault, 132–138, 204–205
jury recommendations, 18, 19,
      20–21
    Conter murder, 27–28

K

Kaplan, Robert, 30–31, 41
Keele Centre, 12
Keeler, Terrence, 31–32

Kelleher, James, 27–28

Kenneth, sex offender, 75–76

Kingston Penitentiary (KP), 1, 2, 16, 17, 28, 29
  E Block, 44–47
  Regional Treatment Centre, 64
  and rehabilitation programs, 47–56
  and sex offender treatment program, 38

Kingston Psychiatric Hospital, 6

Kingston, Sexual Behaviour Clinic, 68–78, 91, 95, 166–167
  and deviant proclivities, 186–187
  funding for, 201
  1979 study, 114–115
  recidivism and child molesters, 180–181
  study on pornography, 157, 174–175

Kirkpatrick House, 25, 27

Kocurek, Paul, 29–30

Koenig, Joseph, 98

Kutchinsky, Beryl, 171

L

Langevin, Ron, 93

Lavoie-Roux, Thérèse, 141

Law Union of Ontario, 138

Lerner, M.J., 111

Levine, Sylvia, 98

Lewis, Dorothy, 155

lie detector tests, 127

Longarini, Peter, 38, 40

Loyola University of Chicago 1986 study, 115

M

McCarthy, Vincent, 118–119

McGillivray, Chief Justice William, 136

MacIsaac, John, 116, 120–121, 140

McKay, Elmer, 32–33

Malamuth, Neil, 163

Malcolm, Bruce, 47–52

Maletzky, Barry, 194

mandatory supervision, conditions of, 3–4

Manitoba aboriginal justice inquiry, 126, 128–129

Marciano, Georges, 158

Marlatt, Alan, 191

Marques, Janice, 191

Marshall, Bill, 9, 81, 201
  and Duane Taylor, 5–6
  and Kingston Sexual Behaviour Clinic, 53
  and program for sex offenders, 55

Marshall, Patricia, 131

Matsqui federal prison, 29

media:
  and sexual images, 159
  and violence, 207

Messier, Camille, 142–143

Metropolitan Toronto Police, 12
  and Melvin Stanton escape, 22–24
  pornography and hate-literature squad, 160–161

Michaels, Merek David, 40

Miles, Bill, 47, 64–66

Molloy, Reverend Kevin, 116

Montgomery Centre, 12, 23–24, 27, 39

Morrison, April, 7–8, 81

Mount Cashel orphanage, 79, 113, 116, 118–122, 138, 139–140

Mowers, Lonnie Allan, 39, 112–113

Murphy, Anthony, 119–120

N

Nash, Gerald, 121
Nation, 138
National Film Board, 2, 96
National Parole Board, 6, 11, 12,
    26, 63
   and Conter murder, 28
   and legislation, 179–180
   membership of, 35
   and release of Melvin Stanton,
    10
New York Times, 82
Newton, Judge C. James, 59
Nielsen, Erik, 37
Norberg, LeRoy, 140
Noyes, Robert, 85–90, 123–124
Nunziata, John, 26

O

Oakridge Mental Health Centre,
    193
O'Brien, Dereck, 122, 144–145
O'Driscoll, Mr. Justice John, 8
Olson, Clifford, 18, 31, 79–80,
    129–130
   and E Block, 44
   and pornography 155–156
Ontario Coalition of Rape Crisis
    Centres, funding for, 143
Ontario Ministry of Community
    and Social Services, 201
Ontario Ministry of Correctional
    Services, 63, 201
Ontario Ministry of Health, and
    sex offenders, 201
Ontario Provincial Police, 128
Ontario Supreme Court, 8
Ontario Women's Directorate, 138
Ottawa Citizen, 141
Outaouais Youth Protection
    Services, 141

P

parole board, responsibilities of,
    3–4
parole officers, duties of, 40
parole service, 26
passive planning, 192
Patterson, Pat, 11
pedophiles, 81–82
   profile of, 93–94
   Taylor, Duane, 1–9
   see also child molesters
Penney, Alphonsus, 121–122
Penthouse, 161
Pepino, Jane, 23, 63
Peter, child molester, 98
phallometric testing, 70–71, 77,
    93
physical abuse, 118, 120–121
Pithers, Bill, 184, 191, 200
Playboy, 161, 169
police:
   attitudes to victims, 126–131
   training and sexual assault,
    204
pornography:
   as big business, 161–162
   child, 158–160
   and children, 169–170
   definition of, 157–158
   effects on persons, 164–178
   laws governing, 159–161
   link to sexual assault, 154–
    178
   and sexual assault in Denmark,
    171
power imbalances between men
    and women, 167–168
Princeton University, 138
privatization of halfway houses,
    24
professionals, and need for
    support, 152–153

Q

Quebec's Committee of Youth
    Protection, 141–142
Queen's University, 138

R

rape crisis centres, 143
    funding for, 202
rapists, 13–14
    Barnes, Douglas, 37–38
    Brian, 74–75
    Evans, Ross, 38–39
    Fred, 95–96
    Huyghebaert, Andre, 56–62
    Keeler, Terrence, 31–32
    Kocurek, Paul, 29–30
    Stanton, Melvin, 10–18
    Steingard, Kenneth, 18–19
    Sweeney, Allan James, 19–20
    Warren, 76–78
    see also individual names
    profile of, 92–93, 95–106
RCMP, 127, 129
recidivism rate, 180–181, 194–
    195
Regional Psychiatric Centre,
    Kingston, 8
Reid, Peter, 124
relapse prevention strategies,
    190–193
Riche, Chesley, 120
Riverview Psychiatric Hospital,
    16
Robinson, Fernand, and
    pornography, 156
Rogers, Rix, 142
Roman Catholic Church, 79,
    120–123, 196, 198
Ron, child molester, 101–102
Royal Newfoundland
    Constabulary, 119

Royal Ottawa Hospital, 20, 57,
    183
Royal Victoria Hospital, 6

S

Saad, Ali, 15
sadism, 78
sadistic rapists, 92, 93, 172
sadomasochism, 29
Salvation Army, 5, 6
Sanday, Peggy, 206
Saskatoon treatment centre, 53
Seidman, Bonnie, 166–167
serial killers see Bundy, Ted;
    Olson, Clifford
sex offender programs,
    examination of, 63–64
sex offenders:
    Bird, Bruce, 34
    Boden, Wayne, 41
    Evans, Ross, 38–39
    Fletcher, Robert, 32
    Foster, Allan George, 20
    Fowler, James, 41
    Huyghebaert, Andre, 56–62
    James, Bruce John, 33
    Keeler, Terrence, 31–32
    Kenneth, 75–76
    Michaels, Merek David, 40
    Mowers, Lonnie, 39
    Olson, Clifford, 18, 31
    Steingard, Kenneth, 18–19
    Sweeney, Allan James, 19–20
    see also individual names
    and assessment process, 49–52,
        56
    lawsuit against the government,
        57–58
    payment for therapy, 5, 9–10
    profile, 78–84
    and release by parole board,
        35–37

and social status, 79
with subnormal intelligence, 9
treatment programs for, 2–3,
  47–49, 52–56
sexual assault:
  aftermath of, 139–140
  of children, 141–142
  long term effects on victims,
    145–152
  and social attitudes, 108–117,
    126
Sexual Behaviour Clinic, New York
  Psychiatric Institute, 156
sexual dysfunction, 188–189
Simms, Frank, 120
sociobiologist view of rape,
  105–06
Solomon, Bette, 150–151
Stanton, Melvin, 10–18, 23
  and brain surgery, 15
  childhood, 13–14
  and E Block, 46
  escape, 23–24
  rapist, 13–14
  and therapy, 16–17
Statistics Canada, 109, 127–128
Steingard, Kenneth, and
  pornography, 156
Stewart, Graham, 36, 37, 56
Stewart, Lynn, assessment of
  Melvin Stanton, 11
Stienberg, Mac, 12
St. John's *Evening Telegram*, 120
St. Leonard's halfway house, 4
stress management, 189
Strickland, Veronica, 119–120
Sturup, G.K., 183–184
suicidal inmate, 17
suicide rate in prison, 32
suicides, 45
Swank magazine, 160
Sweeney, Allan James, 19–20,
  24–27, 33

T

Taylor, Duane, 1–9, 80–81
temporary absence passes, 10
therapy, payment for, 5, 21
Toronto's Metro Action
  Committee on Public Violence
  Against Women and
  Children, 131
treatment programs, 47–66
treatment of sex offenders:
  castration, 183–184
  cognitive-behavioural method,
    185–188
  drug therapy, 182–183
  effectiveness, 181–189
  and federal government,
    201–202
  and recidivism, 180–181
  single prison approach, 199–200
Trono, Art, 9

U

U.S. National Crime Survey, 115
United States Attorney General's
  Commission on Pornography,
  156–157
United States Commission on
  Obscenity and Pornography,
  173
Urquhart, William, 130

V

Vancouver *Sun*, 30, 127, 129
Vermont Treatment Program for
  Sex Offenders, 184
victims:
  attitudes toward, 110–111,
    126–138
  counselling of, 140
  effects of rape on, 144–146

Victims (*cont'd.*)
  and fighting back, 115
volunteers, and need for support,
  152–153

W

Warkworth penitentiary, 16, 53,
  85
Warren, child molester, 76–78
Wayne, young friend of Robert
  Noyes, 86–87, 90

Weir, John, 34
Whitby Psychiatric Hospital, 6
White, Chief Superintendent Jack,
  127
Why Men Rape, 96, 98
Williams, Sharon, 54–55, 62
Winnipeg School Division, 125
women, and the courts, 206–207

Z

Zillmann, Dolf, 168

ABOUT THE AUTHORS

DR W.L. MARSHALL is a Professor of Psychology and an Associate Professor in the Departments of Psychiatry and Urology at Queen's University in Kingston, Ontario.

He is also Co-director of the Kingston Sexual Behaviour Clinic.

SYLVIA BARRETT is an award-winning journalist who has spent nineteen years working as a writer and editor for daily newspapers and magazines.

THRILLING
FAST-PACED FICTION
FROM SEAL

THE INNOCENT *by Ian McEwan*

SCORPIO MOON *by Kurt Maxwell*

TITANIC *by Tony Aspler*

NIGHTEYES *by G. Reeves-Stevens*

DARK MATTER *by G. Reeves-Stevens*

THE CAT AND THE RAT *by Robert Wall*

DREAMER *by Peter James*

DRACULA UNBOUND *by Brian Aldiss*

THE NINE DRAGONS *by Justin Scott*

100 HORSE *by Marco Soren*

The Mark of Canadian Bestsellers